ADMITTED

AN INTERACTIVE WORKBOOK FOR GETTING INTO A TOP MBA PROGRAM

BETSY MASSAR

WITH

FRANCESCA DI MEGLIO

FOR PHYLLIS

عِلم

Published by 85 Broads
An Exclusive Global Women's Network
www.85broads.com

ISBN-13: 978-0615552125

Printed in the United States of America

Book design by Stacey Aaronson
www.creative-collaborations.com

TABLE OF CONTENTS

INTRODUCTION

The business school application scares most people. Sure, to outsiders, it looks simple enough – fill out a few forms, take a standardized test, send transcripts, answer some essay questions, get recommendations, and voilà, you're in.

If only. Since you are reading this book, you know it is not simple at all. Even deciding whether to apply, or to what schools you should apply, is a challenge. And there are no easy answers.

Part of the problem is that there's an imbalance; you spend hours, if not days or months, wondering whether to interrupt a successful career to spend thousands of dollars on a business education. You study for months for a standardized test that tries to outsmart you. You spend time and energy figuring out which programs appeal most. You travel to visit campuses, cold-call alumni, and corral at least two, maybe three people senior to you to write thoughtful, specific recommendations about your excellence. To add to the indignity of it all, you have to write a set of personal, soul-wrenching essays that justify your decision to attend the program of your choice. Then, there's the probabilistic evidence that less than 10 percent of applicants to your favorite school are admitted.

So, why bother? Because the business school experience can change your life. It is the ticket to a new career and an expanded network. Business school is an amazing opportunity for knowledge and growth; it's fun, and there's a better than even chance that your MBA degree will pay itself back in a relatively few years.

Managing Your Campaign

Admitted is not about the benefits of business school. Instead, it organizes your thoughts so that you can turn in the best application that you are able to put forth, should you decide to go for it. It pushes you to figure out whether, and why, you want to earn an MBA. In fact, in the very first chapter, there's an exercise that questions your resolve to attend business school. It challenges you to figure out whether you really want to go down this path. After all, if you don't want to attend business school, you'll be wasting the year or so it takes to prepare the application, and then, of course, the lost years of income while you are in school.

Once you decide to jump into the business school application, this workbook can help you navigate the process. It's here to help you structure your campaign and encourage you to think long and hard about your aspirations, experience, work style, emotional intelligence, and place in the world.

Along with helpful tips and stories about successful applicants, *Admitted* breaks down the application journey from beginning to end. The first few exercises on preparation may be simple for those who are absolutely committed to getting started with applications and are raring to go. Even so, the exercises encourage you to take a step back and test yourself on what you really want and what you hope to get out of the MBA experience. Whether the "Why MBA?" question is asked overtly on the application, or whether it comes up in an interview, the people deciding on your candidacy need to understand what has drawn you to business school and what role the degree will play in your ultimate goals. When the competition is so stiff, those who build a class are going to absolutely favor the students who really know why they want to be there over those who are still trying to figure it all out.

As you explore and try on different MBA programs for size, *Admitted* serves as your guide. Instead of telling you what school fits, the exercises in the book encourage and challenge you to ask the important questions that will help you decide what fits and importantly, what does not.

The workbook also has exercises for you to dissect your work history and create compelling stories about what you've achieved. Admissions officers want to see that you've taken advantage of every opportunity on the job and in your extracurricular life. They want to see that you have taken charge and made things happen for yourself and your organization.

The exercises and templates in the following chapters will give you tools to make your stories compelling and relevant to the questions asked on the application and by potential interviewers.

A Framework to Tackle the Essays

There's nothing worse than staring at a blank computer monitor and trying to come up with your three most significant accomplishments or justification for your short- and long-term career goals.

Not surprisingly, one of the most frequent laments of aspiring MBA students is, "How do I figure out how to answer the questions?"

Exercises in *Admitted* help you to articulate your goals and dreams and the reasons you feel motivated to do what you do. Just like with the MBA essay questions, **in this workbook, you can give no right or wrong answers.** That's because only you, and maybe your close circle of friends, family, and mentors, really know what is authentic for you. Everyone's story is unique, thank heavens; after all, the admissions committees never want to hear canned responses, nor do they want to sit through the same boring answer over and over again.

Many students think there is some magical response for every essay question and piling the pixie dust onto the application will result in guaranteed acceptance. It doesn't. Admissions committees can see manufactured answers from a great distance. That's because there are no easy answers. You are in charge of "your one wild and precious life," as poet Mary Oliver calls it. The decisions you have made are your very own, and those decisions are what admissions committee members want to know about. They want to know what drives you and what values you hold dear. They want to know what makes you get up in the morning and work late at night. They want to know what it is that makes you so very, very interesting. And that's why they ask such open-ended questions.

The Questions behind the Questions

The exercises in this workbook are designed to help you answer the questions behind the questions. When a school asks you about your career vision or leadership or ability to work in teams, it is looking for more than a linear reply. It is giving you a platform to justify why you are the right candidate for a seat in the next matriculating class.

Completing the exercises in this workbook will help you articulate that profound assertion. Some of what you write won't make any sense at first. But the creative part of your brain works in mysterious ways, and you may find that one question inspires a wisp of an idea that might answer another question, and that might become the building block for another essay entirely. Or it may provide some inspiration that you had never expected.

It helps if you approach the application process with an open mind. Begin the process as you would a journey. Take yourself seriously, but not too seriously. Look for clues in your past and present that will help you explain why you are who you are, at this very moment, applying to a particular school. And why, of course, they should admit you. Prepare to be enlightened and even surprised by what you find out about yourself.

How this Book is Organized

Let's be honest. You don't have to read the whole workbook, and you certainly don't have to do every exercise. In fact, if you do just a few exercises, and they inspire you to get up and start networking, visiting campuses, or drafting your goals essay, then it's worth it. Clearly some sections will make more sense to you than others. For your convenience, as you pick and choose the sections that will best help you, each chapter is summarized below.

Admitted is divided into eight chapters:

1. Preparation

There's always more to do than you think. This chapter helps you get all your ducks in a row, figure out what you need to do before you get started, or if you've already started, it helps you figure out what you might have overlooked. Importantly, it tests your rationale for going to business school, and helps you prepare your response to the question that you will be asked in the application, in your interview, by your friends and family, and by those you choose to write your recommendations: "Why do you want an MBA?" In this section, you'll also learn how to define and organize your network, so that you can choose the program that fits you and your goals best.

2. Filling in the Gaps

Before you apply, it's important to know where you may stand. Fortunately, business schools publish profiles of the most recently admitted class, so you can compare your undergraduate grades and test scores and see how you measure up. This section offers tips on how to analyze your profile and suggests ways you can fill in gaps if necessary.

3. Work Experience

Business school admissions committees want to see that you have progressed in your career, made deliberate choices, and are going in a specific direction (forward, we hope). This section tutors you in analyzing your career history and gives you clues on how to write about your experiences. A resume template and a storytelling tool called "the hero's model," a classic paradigm that has worked for centuries – from the myths of ancient Greece to modern video games – round out the section.

4. Extracurricular Activities: Mining Your History for the Out-of-the-Ordinary

Extracurriculars are helpful not just to show that you are interested in community service – in fact, some of your activities may be purely for fun. And that's fine. What's important is that you prove you're well-rounded, and this section teaches you how to talk about your leadership and teamwork experiences outside of work. Representatives from the Harvard Business School have noted that they are looking for a "habit of leadership" in potential candidates. If you don't work for a company where you are promoted to CEO by the time you apply, you can use your leadership skills as captain of a sports team or organizer of a junior karate championship. Discover how you can draw upon your leadership and teamwork experiences to round out your application and give color to the kind of person you are in real life.

5. The Essays

Work experience and extracurriculars warm you up for the big essay questions, which ask, in essence:

Why You? Why the MBA? Why Now?

The essays are the heart of the application. Certainly some schools' essay questions are scarier than others – take, for example, that of Stanford Graduate School of Business: "What is most important to you and why?" The answers to these questions require a great deal of self-reflection, and this section helps piece together your answers.

Admissions officers are looking for examples of your character, influence, teamwork, and leadership. The exercises in this section will help you identify certain traits and experiences about which you will want to write. This section asks you to look at your decisions, motivations, attitudes, and aspirations. It asks you about whom you influence and who influences you; it asks you what you are good at and what you could be better at. It then looks at leadership and emotional intelligence, teamwork, resiliency, risk taking, and giving and receiving feedback.

6. Recommendation Wrangling

Admissions committees look at recommendation letters far more closely than you may imagine. So it's important to choose your recommenders carefully and to prep them well in advance. In fact, selecting and briefing those who will write your recommendation letters is so important that you should schedule this activity in the early part of your timetable. Once you set your target admissions round, you should give your recommender a two- to three-month lead time. This chapter comes after the essay deep-dive because the information you will provide the recommender will come, in part, from the material in the previous three chapters. With templates to guide the recommender, this chapter allows you to share examples of your leadership and teamwork with tangible, measurable results. In this section, you will also have a chance to figure out how the recommender should discuss your weaknesses or areas of development.

7. Prep for the Interview

This chapter gives you the tools and exercises to review and clarify your story and to make it succinct and believable. You'll be asked to review parts of your application and some of the stories you may want to add. You'll also find suggestions for questions to ask the interviewer and a mock interview evaluation form to give your practice partner. Because yes, you have to practice.

8. The Waiting is the Hardest Part

By the time you get to this chapter, you probably won't want anything more to do with the application. This section simply reminds you that you have interests beyond applying to business school, and you have friends and family who want to know how you are doing. It also tells you that it's okay to be anxious; anyone would be in your shoes.

Final Note

This workbook has been a labor of love. It started out as an idea over lunch with a colleague and turned into what you are reading right now. Everyone approaches business school applications differently, and you are right to do so. You'll figure out what works for you. All I hope is that this workbook gives you a way to put your best self forward before the admissions committee.

You deserve it.

Betsy Massar
Oakland, CA

ADMITTED

CHAPTER I: PREPARATION

START EARLY!

Applying to graduate school is like a campaign. You have a goal and you need to organize your actions to achieve that goal. This means mapping out a strategy, planning each step, juggling all the moving parts, executing, following up, and all while performing your day job. You will need to use your powers of persuasion to secure help from friends, family, and potential recommenders. You will also need to do a bunch of things at the same time, like study for your GMAT or GRE, meet current students and alumni, explore career paths, take extra courses, ask for transcripts, reflect on your own goals, oh, and figure out how to pay for the privilege of going to school.

To help make your campaign for the MBA a success, I've created this workbook. It's intended to help you navigate your way through the application process from beginning to end by prompting you to think about this big investment and the dedication and skills you bring to the table. You can start most of the activities listed below before you apply. But you will also want to carry on these activities over the weeks, months, and yes, *years* you might spend pondering the application questions, meeting people and eliciting feedback, attending workshops and fairs, and visiting schools.

THERE'S MORE TO DO THAN YOU THINK

The earlier you start thinking about the process, the easier it will be to put it all together. I've never met a candidate who said afterward, "That was a lot easier and took a lot less time than I thought!"

You'll find many benefits to starting the process early. There's no downside. Those who start early will be able to take the time to do all the work and self-reflection that's required to make a successful application to business school. You'll be able to clarify your purpose and challenge yourself to see if getting an MBA is right for you. You'll be

> *You'll be able to start thinking about how you have shown a pattern of leadership, and if you need to fill in the gaps, you'll have time to do so.*

able to start thinking about how you have shown a pattern of leadership, and if you need to fill in the gaps, you'll have time to do so. You can take extra courses, immerse yourself in community activities, attend workshops, such as Stanford's Many Voices and XX Factor Sessions or the Duke MBA Weekend for Women. If you plan in advance, you may be able to visit schools in the spring term, when class is in session and students are more seasoned (and less pressured).

Stanford's Many Voices and XX Factor sessions:
http://www.gsb.stanford.edu/mba/admission_events/us_minorities.html

Duke MBA Weekend for Women:
http://www.fuqua.duke.edu/programs/duke_mba/daytime/apply_daytime/weekend_for_women/

Carrie* came to one of my pre-MBA essay workshops a year before she intended to apply to programs. She told me later that she found the exercises that got her thinking about her uniqueness as a person and leader to be most helpful. Nevertheless, as a practical matter, she needed to get her GMAT score up, since she received a 590. So, she spent the next year (when she wasn't at work) studying a rigorous GMAT course. She also found a book on test anxiety and worked through those exercises.

APPLICANT PROFILE

By the time she took the test, she was ready, focused, and calmer than she had been the first time. Her new score was 700. She was admitted to four of the five schools to which she applied, including Northwestern University's Kellogg School of Management, where she will be matriculating.

Despite beginning her business school quest more than one year in advance, she still feels she could have done more research had she started even earlier: "I think I would have visited more programs," she said. "It really does give you a feel for whether you'd be a good fit, and if your background and experiences can compete with the student body."

 EXERCISES

Before you start looking at business schools, imagining yourself behind a big desk on Wall Street, or launching your own business with degree in hand, you should determine if the MBA truly is the right path for you. The truth of the matter – and something an admissions committee may be reluctant to tell you – is that not everyone needs an MBA to accomplish his or her goals. For some, the degree is simply not the right choice.

While that's true, education always stretches the mind and opens you up to new experiences. But investing in a graduate business program brings with it hefty tuition and, if you go full time, a two-year halt to your career. The very first step in the application process is, therefore, making sure it is worth it for you.

* All the names of students have been changed for anonymity.

WHY BUSINESS SCHOOL?

List reasons ANYONE might go to business school – without making any value judgment. Here are a few for starters:

1. To get a better job
2. To make more money
3. To make friends/network
4. To have more interesting work
5. To change careers
6. To expand horizons

What might be some other reasons? Write them below. Remember, these reasons do not have to apply to you, just any reason you may have heard of.

7. _____
8. _____
9. _____
10. _____
11. _____
12. _____

Now, look at all the reasons above. Do any of these resonate? Now, pick your top five most important reasons. Don't worry about the order.

1. _____
2. _____
3. _____
4. _____
5. _____

When talking about the reasons for going to business school, students often mention the opportunity to improve their knowledge, skills, and abilities.

? Ask yourself the following questions to determine if you should indeed pursue an MBA:

Are you looking for strategic/decision making, management, or technical/operational skills? What kind?

_____

_____

_____

_____

RESERVATIONS

Anyone who is weighing an important decision realizes there are risks. It's also fair to have reservations. List below some reasons why you might not want to go to business school. Here are a few to get you started:

Reasons to skip or postpone an MBA program:

1. Timing
2. Money
3. Cost outweighs benefit
4. Not committed enough
5. Resistance from family/friends
6. Good career path at work

7. _____

8. _____

9. _____

10. _____

Do any of those reasons resonate? If so, why?

_____

_____

_____

_____

_____

Do you think the pros outweigh the cons?

☐ Yes ☐ No

...Chances are you think the pros outweigh the cons, or you wouldn't be looking at a book like this. But the application process is not for the faint of heart.

What could change your mind? A life event? A promotion? Worries about finances? Just not sure of the right path yet?

_____

_____

_____

_____

_____

_____

? ASK YOURSELF

Are you the one who really wants the MBA, or is there some other outside force at work? You want to be honest with yourself. Who is driving this decision? Who (if anyone) are you trying to impress by getting an MBA?

- Your father or mother
- Your ex-boss
- Your ex-boyfriend or girlfriend
- Your junior high school math teacher
- Your potential boss
- Your annoying cousin
- A McKinsey recruiter
- Jamie Dimon

- _____
- _____
- _____

Jamie Dimon
Chairman and CEO of JPMorgan Chase

Reflect on what earning an MBA would bring to your professional life and do for you personally. Give yourself time. Then jot down your thoughts envisioning the future, the potential and possible fruit of your labor.

_____

_____

_____

_____

_____

_____

_____

_____

_____

_____

_____

_____

_____

_____

APPLYING TO THE RIGHT BUSINESS SCHOOL - FOR YOU

Now that you've determined that the MBA can help you make your dreams come true, you can start thinking about the schools to which you would like to apply. As I've mentioned before, it makes sense to start early in this process so you can refine your choices and also learn a bit more about yourself on the way. You can use this time to research, network, pick up valuable work experience, visit campuses, and, believe it or not, have a good time.

RESEARCHING SCHOOLS

Here are some things you can do to learn about where you might want to go to business school:

- ✦ Go to MBA fairs and school-sponsored outreach events
  In person (preferable)
  Online (easier to schedule and are increasingly available)
- ✦ Talk to current students
- ✦ Talk to alumni
- ✦ Sign up for outreach programs. Examples include UCLA's Riordan Fellows Program or the Kellogg Women's Leadership Workshop, or the aforementioned Duke and Stanford programs (plus, too many more to list here)
- ✦ Visit schools
- ✦ Read school websites
- ✦ Read student blogs
- ✦ Watch YouTube videos on schools – official and non-official
- ✦ Follow/like school pages on Twitter – or better yet, Facebook
- ✦ Check out the list of chats and events at the MBA.com website (the GMAT people), Bloomberg BusinessWeek, admission consultant websites, and reputable MBA portals
  - ★ Don't fall into scare tactics of some who claim on Internet forums and in some news articles that they have an inside edge on who gets in and who will get dinged. *Nobody* has that information.
- ✦ Talk to your career mentor
- ✦ Talk to friends and relatives you respect
- ✦ Take notes!

Keep an open mind when you are researching. You never know what you will find as schools, programs, and career trends are changing all the time.

Some applications and interviewers ask you what you have done to learn about the program. The answer will not make or break your candidacy. However, if you are applying to UC Berkeley Haas, and live across the bridge in San Francisco but have never set foot on campus, it could be an issue. Furthermore, with so many channels available such as fairs, outreach programs, student ambassadors, clubs, blogs, Facebook, Skype, Twitter, you name it – it's hard to find an excuse **not** to have talked directly to students, alumni, or school reps. It's good to have an action plan.

📄 List here what steps you will take to research programs:

1. _____

2. _____

3. _____

4. _____

5. _____

6. _____

7. _____

8. _____

9. _____

10. _____

🖱 Riordan programs:
http://www.anderson.ucla.edu/x1326.xml

🖱 Kelllogg Women's Leadership Workshop:
http://www.kellogg.northwestern.edu/wlw/

TALK TO PEOPLE IN YOUR TARGET CAREER

Ask for honest feedback about the role of the MBA in the career. Be prepared for them to say the degree isn't required to get ahead. If they say they don't think it is required, what does that mean for your reasons to get an MBA? Write about the reasons why you still want to go for the degree.

_____

_____

_____

_____

_____

_____

_____

_____

_____

_____

_____

_____

DIFFERENTIATING PROGRAMS – CREATING YOUR OWN CHECKLIST

As you probably know, rankings are compiled by publications on a variety of metrics. The ranking organization's algorithm may very well weigh data points that are irrelevant to you. For example, if you want to be an entrepreneur, starting salaries for graduates shouldn't matter. If you want to go to school in New York, Stanford's position on the list shouldn't matter. So, figure out your own criteria.

Put a "1" for important, "2" for maybe important, and "3" for not important next to each criterion (Try to keep the list of "importants" to a reasonable number).

_____	Class size
_____	School size
_____	Faculty interaction
_____	Well-known faculty research
_____	Courses to prepare you for your target industries or functions
_____	Career placement in your target industries
_____	Social life at school
_____	Reputation for teamwork or competitiveness
_____	Near a big city
_____	In a certain region
_____	Starting salaries for graduates
_____	Alumni network
_____	Joint-degree programs
_____	Program cost
_____	Part-time availability
_____	Executive MBA availability
_____	Learning style (for example, classroom, case method, field work)
_____	Program length (one year versus two)
_____	Ability to take courses elsewhere in the university
_____	Other: _____

Now list all of your #1's here:

1. _____

2. _____

3. _____

4. _____

5. _____

6. _____

Keep this list handy when you research schools. You will find that many schools make similar claims, but if you do your research, you will be able to discern the nuances among the schools. Ask questions that will help you understand whether you fit. You may also find that this list will change as you continue to research programs.

 ## EXERCISE

This one comes with a special bonus because it can cure you of writer's block, if you have it. Make a list of dream schools. Feel free to add extra lines, if you wish.

1. _____

2. _____

3. _____

4. _____

5. _____

6. _____

Pick one – any one, just to get you going.

Now, on the next page, write a *very* short story in which you are the hero at this school. As you write, address the following:

- Where are you physically?
- What are you doing?
- What are you talking about?
- Who are you with?

Your story:

_____

_____

_____

_____

_____

_____

_____

_____

_____

_____

_____

_____

_____

_____

_____

_____

_____

_____

_____

_____

_____

_____

_____

_____

_____

STARTING THE CAMPAIGN – GO ON A LISTENING TOUR

Now is the time to ask questions, learn, and network. These activities will not only be part of your application process, but will be part of your daily life at business school and beyond. Even if you end up changing your mind, putting off the decision, or getting sucked into the vortex of work, networking and talking will open up new avenues and might find you a new career, apartment, girlfriend, or boyfriend.

Purposeful networking will connect you with people who can help you decide when/if to go to business school, clarify your reasoning in the application process, or introduce you to students and alumni who might have information that can help.

NETWORKING

Make an Excel worksheet or fill in the form on p. 17 of your first-level LinkedIn connections. You can also do this with Facebook or just your contact list. I like LinkedIn because it is not just social, and it focuses more on your professional life.

In the column next to each name, write briefly how he or she might be able to inform you about the road to graduate school, the career path that interests you, or leadership lessons.

 Blanks are ok. Not everyone needs to be contacted, and you don't have to contact them all at once. Just realize that you have more resources than you know.

Example: Betsy's Abbreviated LinkedIn List:

Name	Relationship (optional)	Reason for staying in touch	Notes/where they can help you
David	undergraduate classmate	works at interesting marketing company	unusual career path, can advise
Michelle	met at a workshop	2nd year at Haas	can advise on school fit
Gabe	met at a networking event	expert in biotech	knows startups and lots of CEOs in health care
Joy	former colleague	works at non-profit	lots of experience in for-profit and non-profit
Rachel	member of alumni group	going to Ross this year	was non-traditional candidate, can advise
Nate	former colleague	Now in brand management	switched from finance to Internet-related

APPLICANT PROFILE

Monique, who lives in a city in Africa that will not be visited by any business schools this year, has combed through her target school websites for African graduates and students, connected with people from her undergraduate alma mater who went to business school, and is using Facebook to find names of current business school students or recent graduates, who might be in her country over the summer.

She also made connections through other networks, such as 85 Broads (www.85broads.com), a global community of professional women. The networks yielded fruit, introducing her to men and women who could advise her on her choices and career options.

YOUR sample LinkedIn List:

Name	Relationship (optional)	Reason for staying in touch	Notes/where they can help you

CAMPUS VISITS

This is the part where deciding whether to go to business school – and which one – can be really fun. If you start early, you will be able to plan well enough in advance to visit schools during the spring semester, when most students have figured out the lay of the land, the weather is better in most places, and life is a bit more relaxed. If you go to a class, you'll get a better sense of camaraderie among the students, who, by then, know each other pretty well. The more relaxed the students, the more enjoyable the experience for you, the visitor. As you plan for this visit, remember, you are the customer. It's a cool position to be in because, at this stage, the school is trying to sell itself to you.

CHECKLIST FOR PLANNING YOUR CAMPUS VISIT:

☐ Is the school in session when you are going?

☐ Is the admissions office holding information sessions?

☐ Will you be able to meet with an admissions officer (if you want to)?

☐ Will you be able to talk to someone in the financial aid office?

☐ Will you be able to sit in on a class?
   - Check available class offerings. Are there any classes that you really want to know about? What are they?

   _____

   _____

   _____

   _____

☐ Will you be able to meet students informally, say over lunch?

☐ Do you know anyone at the school? Will he or she be able to show you around and give you the inside scoop?

☐ Will you be able to find students who have a similar background to you?

☐ Will you be able to find students who have similar career goals to yours?

☐ Will you be able to get a sense of the school's non-academic offerings? How?

_____

_____

_____

_____

_____

☐ Are there any centers or organizations that you want to check out, such as a center on entrepreneurship or leadership? Can you organize this part of the visit in advance, so that there's someone with whom you can talk?

☐ If you have a spouse or partner, can you arrange to meet some people in the same situation as you?

☐ Will you remember to take notes on your impressions of the school, so that you can use that information as you make the case for yourself in the application essays?

☐ Will you also remember to thank and stay in touch with the people you met while you were visiting the school?

APPLICANT PROFILE

Rachel had only wanted to go to school in a temperate climate. But the University of Michigan Ross School of Business' emphasis on environmental sustainability and its reputation for action-based learning convinced her to do a school visit. She thought, what's the downside? In the end, she was so comfortable at Ross that it became her first choice, and she turned down four other offers, including several with financial aid.

AMBIANCE

Make time to check out the school's environment. For example, if you are not sure about how you would feel about living in Hanover, New Hampshire (the location of Dartmouth's Tuck School of Business), spend more than one day there and see if it really is as remote as you think. Other schools might not feel as in the middle of things as you imagine. Kellogg and Stanford GSB require some effort to get into a major city. Also, consider the environment, your spouse's situation, and the living arrangements.

Consider also the resources and feeling of the entire university and the way it integrates with the town. One of my personal favorite towns is Ithaca, New York, home of Cornell University. It is such a beautiful and welcoming college town that's just plain cool. Same for Ann Arbor, Michigan, home of University of Michigan, and the splendid Charlottesville, Virginia, home of the University of Virginia, designed by US President Thomas Jefferson.

Alternatively, some schools are right in the heart of the city. New York University's Stern School of Business feels very "downtown." Walk around Washington Square, imagine yourself living in an apartment nearby, and see if that environment is right for you.

If you don't have time to do all of the above, or if some of the suggestions are irrelevant, skip them. Importantly, prioritize. You will have to choose between many activities (and studying or sleeping) when you are in business school, so you may as well get used to it now.

> **BIT OF ADVICE**
>
> Andrew was accepted to Oxford, thinking (erroneously) that he could commute to the Saïd full-time program from London, where he had moved to be with his new wife. While visiting the school after applying, he found out that he was required to live much closer to campus because the commute from London was time consuming, exhausting, and would take time away from study groups and student activities. He ended up reconsidering his choices and re-applied to only local programs the following year.

FOR THOSE UNABLE TO VISIT CAMPUS

Not everyone will have the opportunity to take a road trip to all of his or her target schools. If you're in that boat, your job is to get as much information as you can through school reps, alumni, and current students who come through your region. You can also find an amazing amount of information virtually. Not only do schools have official YouTube pages, but students love to make videos of themselves at school. B-school shows and annual follies can tell you a surprising amount about the school's culture, if you can stand all the inside jokes.

✎ EXERCISE

Revert to your list of networking resources from p. 17. Make a list of questions that you think will help you get a feel for life at that school. On the following pages are some suggested categories. Given your own situation, you may have a different group of important questions you want answered.

Classroom experience

1. _____

2. _____

3. _____

Student/faculty relations

1. _____

2. _____

3. _____

Student/student relations

1. _____

2. _____

3. _____

Diversity of students and viewpoints

1. _____

2. _____

3. _____

Career management resources

1. _____

2. _____

3. _____

Student activities

1. _____
2. _____
3. _____

Living arrangements

1. _____
2. _____
3. _____

Community and off-campus life

1. _____
2. _____
3. _____

Now go out and get answers, and have fun doing so!

ADMITTED

CHAPTER 2: FILLING IN THE GAPS

GRADES AND SCORES
Your undergraduate record

Assessing your merits – from the grades you earned in college to your standardized test scores – is a necessary and sometimes humbling part of the application process. Fear not. If you don't like what you see, there are things you can do to demonstrate your true potential and encourage admissions committees to see the best version of you. This part of the workbook will help you analyze your grades and scores and determine whether you need to further demonstrate you can handle the academic rigor of an MBA program.

STUFF YOU NEED

Your undergraduate transcript

Order your full transcript from your undergraduate institution(s). You want to look at it in all its glory and see what admissions officers may see. Use the exercises listed to analyze your transcript(s).

☆ Your overall GPA is less relevant than you might think. More important is the trend. What is your GPA by year?

Freshman   _____
Sophomore   _____
Junior   _____
Senior   _____

For those who are not math or hard science majors:

☆ Analyze your performance in various classes, especially the following:

Undergraduate math and or business statistics courses

Calculus grade   _____

Business Statistics grade   _____
     (note: social science statistics grades are not a substitute for business statistics grades)

Economics grades   _____,   _____
     (especially microeconomics or econometrics)

Decision Sciences grade   _____

Finance grade   _____

Accounting grade   _____

Other relevant courses:

_____   _____

_____   _____

_____   _____

_____   _____

? If you earned less than a B in any course, would you consider retaking it?
☐ Yes   ☐ No

Why wouldn't you retake the class?

_____

_____

? If you don't retake a class (and get an A), what other aspects of your application mitigate the low grade on your transcript? Are you sure you don't want to make up for the low grade?

_____

_____

_____

? Do you have any transcript red flags, such as D's or F's?

You will probably have to explain them in the "optional" section. Can you balance the effect of those grades by taking another course? Which one?

_____

_____

Questions for **math**, **engineering**, and **hard science** majors only:

Did you have any real weak spots in your quantitative classes?

☐ Yes   ☐ No

If so, will they weigh against you compared to other applicants who majored in your field?

☐ Yes   ☐ No

If no, why not?

_____

_____

_____

_____

In what courses did you get below a B?

_____

_____

_____

_____

_____

_____

Other than explaining it in the optional section, what else can you do to de-emphasize the weak grades? You might want to take a course in something completely different to show that you are balanced. For example, the engineer who studied poetry is more interesting than someone who never took a humanities class.

? Can you think of any courses in other subjects, such as non-fiction writing or organizational behavior, which might balance your weak spots?

_____

_____

_____

_____

_____

COURSES THAT WORK FOR YOU

If you are in the United States, check your local state school extension program. For example, when I was applying, I decided to make up for my lack of prerequisites by taking seven courses from the University of Virginia's extension program in the D.C. area. I have seen candidates who have done well at other continuing education classes, such as those of the University of California, Hunter College in New York, Harvard, or the Graham School at the University of Chicago.

> _Don't fall for unaccredited schools that advertise all over the Internet._

If you are overseas or traveling a lot, an **online course from an accredited school** may work for you. Don't fall for unaccredited schools that advertise all over the Internet. Try schools that are real, such as major state schools or well-known institutions such as Boston University, Brigham Young University, Johns Hopkins University, Indiana University, or the University of North Carolina. Also, take the course for credit because you want an official transcript. You'd be surprised what an extra document from a real school with lots of A's can do.

But if you already have a pretty good GPA (3.4 or above) from a strong undergraduate program, you might want to supplement your academic experience with some quantitative or business stats courses that do not give you a college-level grade.

For those who think they are deficient in any kind of quantitative courses, the **MBAMath** program might be for you. **MBAMath** is a self-paced online course that is also recommended by a number of MBA programs for students who are already admitted. I like the program because it allows you to make lots of mistakes. The program's philosophy is "getting it right eventually, rather than getting it right the first time." You do get a form of a transcript, which might counterbalance poor grades, but it's not a traditional college course.

If you have no business experience at all and want to challenge yourself, you might want to look at the **MBA IQ** course, an approximately 10-hour online course to prepare students for the MBA classroom, with modules in accounting, operations, finance, strategy, marketing, and more. If you would like a more in-depth program, the same organization offers the **Certified Associate Business Manager (CABM)** designation.

APPLICANT PROFILE

Jenna majored in psychology at Harvard, got very good grades, but hadn't taken any quantitative courses. She wanted to prove that she would be able to sit in an MBA classroom and keep up, but wasn't so worried about the grade because she already had a great track record. She researched a number of courses and decided to take the Managerial Economics module through **Tuck's Online Bridge Program**, which is designed, as it says on the school's website, "for recent liberal arts graduates, PhDs, and other high-potential employees with little or no business education or experience." By completing the class, Jenna hopes to be able to gain a good understanding of business statistics, which comprise some of the basic skills she will have to draw upon in the hectic first term of MBA classes.

SOME RELEVANT LINKS

Please note that these are not the only courses that are available to you – just some that are up and running right now. Keep an eye out for new courses, but remember, before giving anyone your money, check out whether the course is accredited or has an established reputation.

🖱 Tuck Online Business Bridge Program
http://www.tuck.dartmouth.edu/exec/open_programs/online_bridge.html

🖱 MBA Math
http://www.mbamath.com

🖱 MBA IQ
https://mbaiq.com

🖱 Certified Associate Business Manager (CABM)
https://www.apbm.org/?page_id=35

Add new courses here as you find them:

_____

_____

_____

_____

_____

_____

_____

_____

_____

BRAINSTORM WITH YOURSELF

If you do not have a stellar academic record, and you think you have time to make up for the lost years, brainstorm anything else you can do to demonstrate your aptitude. Remember, we are looking for ways to show that you can excel in a competitive classroom.

List possible academic ideas here:

1. _____

2. _____

3. _____

4. _____

5. _____

GMAT/GRE

Should you take the GMAT or the GRE? The GMAT or GRE choice is entirely up to you. Some will debate the merits of each, but in actuality, the most important thing you need to do is figure out whether the school of your choice requires one or the other. In terms of business school, policies on which exam to take are evolving. Check with the Educational Testing Service's GRE programs to see if the schools you wish to apply to will accept GRE scores.

http://www.ets.org/gre/general/about/mba/programs/

Whether you opt for the GMAT or GRE, some of you will at least consider taking a prep course or hiring a tutor. This can be costly, so weigh your options. The road to the highest possible standardized test score is different for everyone. Here's a little exercise to decide whether you should get professional studying help.

In the spirit of full disclosure, I benefited from all sorts of help when I set out to take the GMAT. I had gotten in the fiftieth percentile when I took my undergraduate SATs, and I was understandably petrified about taking the GMAT. But I accessed all the resources I could, including a behavioral eye doctor, who helped me overcome some visual problems that were getting in the way of my performing well on standardized tests. I was scared into several years' training, but it was worth it. My GMAT results came in at the 93rd percentile, with roughly even math and verbal scores.

1. Do you know what the average or median score is for the most difficult school to which you will apply? (Or, if the school reports it as "80 percent of our entering class received between 650 and 750," that's ok.) The information is in the "Class Profile" page. Put that information down here.

    Example: *Kellogg: average 713. Approximately 95% of class of 2012 scored 650 or higher.*

    School: _____

    Average Score: _____

    _____ % of class scored _____ or higher

2. Go to one of the websites that converts those scores to percentiles.

    Example: *Kellogg average: 93rd percentile, minimum: 79th percentile.*

    School: _____

    Average Percentile: _____

    Minimum Percentile: _____

3. Now, go back to the highest SAT score you earned when you were applying to college. Convert those into percentiles – the College Board site has a table at:

    🖰 http://professionals.collegeboard.com/profdownload/sat-percentile-ranks-2010.pdf

Score _____ Percentile _____

Quant percentile _____

4. Compare your SAT percentiles with your target school percentiles. Did you beat the median percentile for your top-choice schools? If so, then you probably don't need to spend money on a full course.

5. If you did not beat the percentile, take a look at the next exercise.

CHOOSE THE RIGHT COURSE

If you did not score around the same percentile that is required OR if you think you are rusty OR you just hate standardized tests in any form, a course is for you. The following questions will help you know what to consider when looking at a test course:

1. Timeframe
    a. How long is it between now and the application deadline? _____

    b. Do you have time to take the test, take a breather, and retake it if you need to improve?　☐ Yes　☐ No

BIT OF ADVICE

If you have more than six months between now and your target application deadline, then you have plenty of choices. This way you can take the test, see how you do, and then study again in areas you need to improve. If you are tight on time, you may want to consider other options, such as an online pre-recorded course, or a private tutor.

2. Do you travel a lot? ☐ Yes ☐ No
    Will you be able to go to a classroom? ☐ Yes ☐ No

> **BIT OF ADVICE**
>
> If you travel a lot, getting to a classroom may be awfully difficult. Don't overestimate your flexibility. Online classes that have a set meeting time may work, especially to keep you disciplined.

3. Is an online "whiteboard" course better for you? ☐ Yes ☐ No

    Obviously, if you are not in a major city, online may make the most sense.

4. Do you do better with individual coaching? ☐ Yes ☐ No

> **BIT OF ADVICE**
>
> You have a wide variety of individual coaches to choose from. You can go private with coaches from any of the major companies or find an individual who is recommended by trusted friends. Some coaches are set up for distance learning, and others are not. Always make sure you and the teacher have a good personality fit and similar goals. Otherwise you are wasting your time and money.

5. Have you researched and compared large companies, different types of courses, and private vendors? ☐ Yes ☐ No

> **BIT OF ADVICE**
>
> Most students underestimate the importance of researching and taking the time to choose the right teaching method. Do not short-change yourself. All providers are **not** equal. Take the time to figure out what is right for you.

> | **TEST ANXIETY** | If you have test anxiety, do not worry. However, you should give yourself an extra six months to study and wrap your brain around the testing process. I highly recommend a personalized tutor in this case as well as study, study, study over a long period of time. For people who are nervous around tests, a class can add to the nervousness because of the fear that you cannot keep up.
>
> A tutor can help you pace your learning, and the right tutor will help you figure out ways to learn from your mistakes efficiently. Not all tutors are equal, and not all tutors need to help you in person. Make sure your tutor, or teacher in a class, uses the right style and methods for you.
>
> Recommended reading: *The Workbook for Test Success*, by Dr. Ben Bernstein, performance coach. More information at:
>
> http://www.workbookfortestsuccess.com

If you have decided to study on your own, list three reasons why you think you will be able to discipline yourself to do so. Really weigh the costs and benefits.

1. _____

2. _____

3. _____

In most cases, your score on the GMAT will depend on:

1. Your test-taking ability
2. The number of months you study
3. The regularity of your studies
4. Your comfort with your coach/teachers
5. Your willingness to learn from your mistakes
6. The quality of the material you study

You have control over all of these items, including number one. But the most important thing you need to do is plan ahead.

CHAPTER 3: WORK EXPERIENCE

Business schools want to know what kind of experiences and skills you'll be bringing to the classroom. After all, the admissions committees build classes, in part, based on what each person adds to the conversation. They're aiming to bring together a diverse group of students who can contribute and educate one another. Indeed, this is precisely why articulating your work experience is so important to the MBA application process. Your goal should be to examine your career progression and determine the best ways to present your track record. Although it may appear indirect at first, this material will help you write your resume and essays and inform the admissions interview.

CAREER PROGRESSION: WARM-UP

While this section is technically the most linear – your career is your career – we want you to look at why you made the decisions you did. Admissions committee members want to know about the decisions that have influenced your life and way of looking at the world. So, to dig deeper into your motivations, your choices, and what you've done with what you've got, I'd like to encourage you to experiment a little. Remember, you are not getting graded on these exercises, so it's now time to break out the crayons and have fun.

You don't have to use a crayon, but it does help to use a fun writing utensil (I prefer fountain pens with colorful ink, myself).

Just jot down some thoughts. You don't have to put your answers in complete sentences. Use this white, unlined space to answer the questions. Like University of Chicago's Booth School of Business' blank pages in its full-time MBA application, there is no right, or even preferred, answer. Go ahead and enjoy it. You can make a collage or simply scribble the answers really fast to get your first thoughts out there. Or, let them roll around in your head for a few days and see what comes up. Don't be afraid to go into the time machine – and go way back – to remember the origins of your decisions.

For example, Deepak realized he wanted to be an engineer because his parents gave him an electric piano to put together when he was 11. And Sarah knew she wanted to be in international trade since her grandparents came back from an overseas trip. Try to make these seemingly obvious questions interesting.

✎ EXERCISES

Why did you decide to:

1.   Take the job you are in now?

2.   Join the industry you are in now?

3.   Apply to business school?

CAREER PROGRESSION: WHY YOU DO WHAT YOU DO

As you probably figured out in the career progression warm-up, these exercises are trying to get you to show some self-awareness about why you have taken and stayed in the job you have now or the jobs you have had in the past. Presumably, you do what you do because you like it, or because you think you can learn something useful from it, or because you are good at it (and it is therefore easier for you than others). Even in jobs you disliked (we've all disliked some jobs), you may have found something you enjoyed. The following exercise will help you figure out what works for you and what doesn't.

Knowing the answers to some of these questions will be helpful as you start thinking about what you want to say about your past successes (and near-misses) and your career and life goals.

 EXERCISES

For each job you have had, answer as many of the following questions as you can. You may not be able to answer all of them for every job, but if you can put down some specifics about your previous experiences, you will have some strong material to inspire great essays.

1.   What did you like the most about your work? How did you make your mark at this job?

_____

_____

_____

_____

_____

_____

_____

2.   How did you take advantage of every opportunity to become a leader at this job?

_____

_____

_____

_____

_____

_____

3.   What kind of formal or informal training did you receive?

_____

_____

_____

_____

_____

_____

4.   What did you like the least about this job?

_____

_____

_____

_____

_____

Repeat for all the significant jobs you have held since graduation from university.

Action plan: What work experience can you get between now and the time you file your application? What gap needs to be filled in? What kind of training can you add?

_____

_____

_____

_____

_____

_____

_____

_____

_____

FRUSTRATION CHECK

Feeling overwhelmed yet? Do you feel as if going back through each job and analyzing it is making you crazy? If you feel that way, you're completely normal. However, going through and taking notes on these past experiences will give rise to ideas that will help you differentiate yourself when you tell your story to MBA admissions officers and interviewers. These wisps of ideas may later generate a story that helps you land a summer internship or a job after graduation.

The best way to come up with stories that you can tell (humbly, of course), is to go back through your own history. Sometimes it doesn't come right away, and sometimes you need to ask your friends and work colleagues. Go through old memos you wrote, and you will often find that you contributed more than you remember.

CAREER PROGRESSION: THE HERO'S MODEL

Before doing the next exercise, you need to understand one of the world's most fundamental story lines, what I call the "hero's model." Most stories in the world are based on myths, and the hero who goes out to slay the monster is one of the oldest. Screenwriters love this story; many of your favorite TV shows, movies, and video games are based on this theme, which was articulated by Joseph Campbell, a comparative mythologist. In his many writings, he talked about the archetypical hero, an everyman who is challenged and changed by his

adventure. Quick web searches will connect Campbell's heroes with Luke Skywalker, Buffy the Vampire Slayer, and Harry Potter, but look deeper and you will find elements of the hero in Ellen Page's character in *Juno* or Finn Hudson in *Glee*.

One way to uncover or mine great stories for your application (and for your next job interview) is to go into your own personal history. This exercise will help you pull out some good nuggets.

Take your resume as it stands now – don't worry about the format – and explore the following on a separate document:

1. Tell the story behind each sentence or bullet point
2. Use the hero's model
3. Spell out your challenge and your solution

Example: *"Revamped a 100-page selling memorandum within three days for a major client on sale of its stake in a European software firm; attracted 28 bidders in the first round"*

a. **Hero**: You

    Explore HOW you arrived at results
    1. Took the time to figure out a plan (skills: ability to strategize, think through a problem)
    2. Pulled in a SWAT team to help – for example, other analysts to run numbers or set up charts and visuals. You may have cajoled, offered pizza, or traded tasks (skills: teamwork, influence, follow-through)
    3. Was able to understand what senior partners needed in the document (skills: managing up, anticipating requirements)

b. **Challenge**: Revamp an important document for a very valuable client in a short period of time

    As with most challenges, you probably had a twist that made the story interesting. For example, in the middle of the process the stock market crashed/a tsunami hit/a subcontractor blew up. You and your team stayed focused and arrived at the result needed.

c. **Result**: Made it attractive to bidders, client happy, company happy

    WIN!

HOW TO TALK ABOUT YOUR CAREER GOALS

While nearly all business schools ask about your career goals, they all know that you may very well change your mind. The question is partly about your ability to plan logically and partly about your ability to envision a wild future. A few pages earlier in the career-progression warm-up, you answered questions about why you want to apply to business school, but you didn't necessarily spell out your specific, minute-by-minute goals. If you work through some of the exercises here, network, and do some introspection, you will become clear on why you want the MBA and where it will get you. Once you figure that out, you will be ready to write the career goal section of your application.

> *If you work through some of the exercises here, network, and do some introspection, you will become clear on why you want the MBA and where it will get you.*

If you want to practice articulating your career goals now, you can skip ahead to p. 137 in chapter 7: Prep for the Interview.

Still, chances are good that as you go through this process you will shift all over the place – and that's all right. It's important to try different ideas on for size. In fact, so many students change their minds from their original career goals that some schools, such as MIT's Sloan School of Management, don't even ask about your goals. Certainly, a transformational experience such as an MBA program will introduce you to ideas and experiences you didn't know were out there.

As an experiment, imagine you are having a conversation with your favorite secondary school teacher. Write down two to three sentences explaining to him or her why you want to go to business school, and describe your broad long-term goals. Use some of what you wrote in the career progression warm-up. (Hint: we will be coming back to this in the recommendation section of the workbook, see chapter 6.)

READING LIST IDEAS

Despite your lack of specifics, you may have some sense of target industries or functions that seem appealing. One of the best ways to research those industries is to read. Find books or articles in your target industries, so you can talk intelligently about the courses or concentrations you might pursue. See if you can get to know the language of the people with whom you will be networking.

For example, if you think you want to go into investment management (hedge funds, private equity) read books about the industry. Popular books include those by Michael Lewis (*Liar's Poker, The Big Short*), Roger Lowenstein (*When Genius Failed, The End of Wall Street*), and Andrew Ross Sorkin (*Too Big to Fail*). There are also lots of books about investment guru Warren Buffett. If you are interested in the quantitative side, try something like *My Life as a Quant* by Emanuel Derman, or Nicholas Taleb's books (*Fooled by Randomness, The Black Swan*).

If you want to go into consulting, read books by Michael Porter (*Competitive Strategy*, for starters) or study the publications of McKinsey, BCG, or Booz & Co. I've heard smart people talk about the book *Good to Great* by Jim Collins as well.

If you are interested in social enterprise, look for books such as *The Blue Sweater*, *The Fortune at the Bottom of the Pyramid*, or anything by Muhammad Yunus. Those with entrepreneurship or start-ups on the brain can read Seth Godin, Geoffrey Moore, or Guy Kawasaki.

Please note that these lists are merely suggestions to help you become fluent in the language of the business you might want to pursue. This kind of reading will help you as you try on different futures. Knowledge and new ideas will make you smarter about yourself and your goals, as well as more self-aware as you answer the questions in the application.

EDUCATE YOURSELF

Do a web search for books on the aforementioned subjects. Look at what bloggers in your industry are reading. See what magazine articles, blog posts, or books professors at your target business schools have published. For example, Chip & Dan Heath, professors at Stanford University and Duke University respectively, show off their research and articles on their academic websites, and on their joint personal website, www.heathbrothers.com, where you can also read about their best-selling books, *Switch* and *Made to Stick*.

Bloomberg Businessweek offers a reading list for business school-bound students, and the *Financial Times* and Goldman Sachs choose an annual business book of the year; any of their nominees are worth reading. The venerable *Harvard Business Review* offers a list of upcoming and notable titles published by the Harvard Business School press.

Relevant links:

🖰 Bloomberg Businessweek B-Schools Reading List:
http://www.businessweek.com/bschools/books/

🖰 Financial Times Business Book of the Year:
http://www.ft.com/intl/indepth/business-book-award-2011

🖰 Harvard Business Review book blog:
http://blogs.hbr.org/synthesis

List here the books/publications you need to look for:

_____

_____

_____

_____

_____

_____

_____

_____

_____

_____

_____

_____

_____

_____

_____

_____

_____

_____

THE RESUME TEMPLATE

You will have to present a resume with your application. It should be one page. Most admissions officers prefer one page as they have lots of reading to do and may resent it if you get carried away.

The template below is relatively standard for business schools. You may lead with your education if you think it is more important than your professional experience. Either will work. If you would like a copy of this template, you may download one at the book's website:

↝ http://www.admittedmba.com

I have heard admissions officers say that the resume is not a list of job duties. It is a record of your accomplishments.

Remember that.

FIRST NAME LAST NAME
Address, City, State Zip/Country Code, Country
Telephone Number   Email Address

Experience

Organization Name   City, State/Country
Brief organization description, if necessary
Job Title   Year Worked – Year Worked
- Brief description of accomplishments, with concrete actions and quantifiable results (3-5 bullet points). If promoted or progressed faster than normal, point it out
- Second bullet point
- Third bullet point
- Fourth bullet point (fourth and fifth bullet points optional)

Job Title   Year Worked – Year Worked
- Brief description of accomplishments, with concrete actions and quantifiable results (3-5 bullet points). If promoted or progressed faster than normal, point it out
- Second bullet point
- Third bullet point

add more jobs if necessary

Education

Institution   City, State/Country
Degree Name, Subject Area   Year Attended – Year Attended
- Academic honors, scholarships, professional/student organizations, and positions of leadership
- More if required

add more education if necessary

Additional

- Language competencies, interests/hobbies
- Technical/computer skills
- Community service

HELPFUL RESUME TIPS

- **Remember the resume is a document of your achievements, not job duties**

- Avoid acronyms and industry jargon

- Try to keep bullet points to no more than two lines, if possible

- Don't feel like you need to use up four or more bullet points – three is fine

- Use 12 or 11-point type, depending on the font you choose. 10-point type can be too small

- Use a clean font, such as Arial, Calibri, Century Gothic, or any other sans serif font

- Leave at least a one-inch margin all the way around to avoid it looking too crowded

- If you held a leadership position in a non-profit, be sure to include it

- You can include only two or fewer bullet points for part-time jobs and internships

- Place education at the bottom if you are working full time and career is the most important; if you are a current student, education leads the resume

CHAPTER 4: EXTRACURRICULAR ACTIVITIES: MINING YOUR HISTORY FOR THE OUT-OF-THE-ORDINARY

Many applicants get confused about the extra-curricular portion of the application. Yes, you do want to show the admissions committee that you are more than just your academics and your work experience. In addition to filling out the worksheets below, you might want to brainstorm with yourself, a friend, or a mentor about activities that show what's interesting about you, flaunt your uniqueness, or demonstrate leadership in a not-so-obvious way.

Try using a template like the one below to fill in your activities and see what comes up.

Activities Since College	Dates	Position	Awards/Notes
GE Internal Newsletter	1/09 – present	Weekly columnist	GE Impact Award
Breast Cancer Awareness	7/10 – present	Runner and fundraiser	Honored as "fundraising hero"
Duke Club of Chicago	6/08 – present	Activities Chair	Held an average of 15 events per year
ESL Tutor	6/09 – 6/10	Tutor/Mentor	Helped Saudi woman get into biology grad school

Activities During College	Dates	Position (if relevant)	Awards/Notes
Swim Team	Soph, Jr, Sr years	Co-captain, senior year	Team came in 2nd in ACC division
Amateur Theatre	Senior yr	Chorus member, "Cabaret"	Most fun of all four years
Explorers Society	Fresh, soph yrs	Member	Hiking, outdoor activities
Community Service, etc			

Now, fill in your own tables. This will help you determine what goes in the data portion of the application, and it will also help you look for patterns of leadership or story ideas for the essays.

Activities	Dates	Position	Awards/Notes

OUTSIDE-THE-BOX HOBBIES

After filling out the exercises on the previous page, you may realize that your list of extracurricular activities, at least since college, might be fairly thin. Let's be serious — what, besides getting into business school, interests you? Outside of formal clubs and organizations, think back to some of the hobbies or other activities in which you might have participated.

First, to get ideas percolating, here is a list of real hobbies and interests I've collected from resumes and applications of some amazing applicants with whom I've worked. Every one of these activities is real:

+ Armchair movie critic
+ Devoted Sacramento Kings fan
+ Earthquake relief
+ Exploring global cuisine
+ Extreme sports on ESPN
+ Fiction writing
+ Hosting parties
+ iPhone app development
+ Jeopardy
+ Jewelry making
+ Pep band
+ Persian art enthusiast
+ Poetry
+ Political affairs
+ Private airplane pilot
+ Sports blogging
+ Wakeboarding
+ Waltzing
+ Wilderness area guide
+ Winemaking
+ Writing and performing comedy

USING YOUR EXPERIENCES TO STRUT YOUR STUFF

Of course, even a traditional hobby/interest can be interesting and show sides of your personality, leadership, and ability to work and play well with others. Have you ever competed at a regional or national level? Or, like in the TV show *Friday Night Lights*, have you felt the whole community's interest resting on your shoulders? Regardless, the story about competition, particularly in a group, can be compelling, funny, interesting, or enlightening. Some archetypical stories (like bringing a team back from defeat) always make for a good essay or interview fodder. You'd be surprised by how many applicants have overcome different kinds of obstacles in their lives. Here are some prompts from real life:

✎ EXERCISES

Have you ever…

1. Shaped up a sports team/work group/volunteer squad from a bunch of irregulars? (Say, for example, the *Glee* choir)

_____

_____

_____

_____

_____

2. Taught yourself something against all odds or defied all normal expectations? (For example: a difficult language, a musical instrument, the CFA, or learning to walk after an accident)

_____

_____

_____

_____

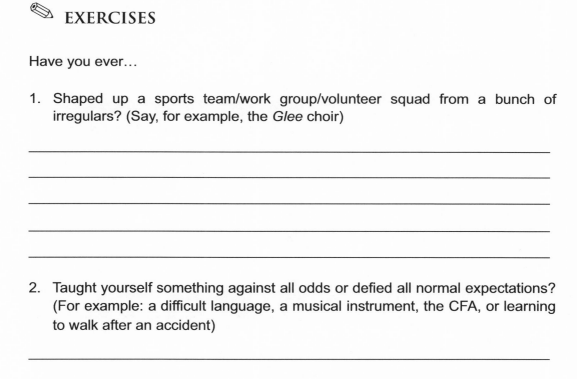

3. Motivated people to do something they would not normally do, such as contribute mightily to a food drive, go surfing, or speak in public?

_____

_____

_____

_____

_____

_____

4. Involved yourself in an activity to conquer a fear, such as becoming a competitive swimmer to get over a fear of water?

_____

_____

_____

_____

_____

_____

5. Been part of a committee or board where no one was on the same page and you worked with everyone to bring them into alignment?

_____

_____

_____

_____

_____

_____

BREAKING THE RULES OF GENDER

It's also interesting when men take up "traditional" women's hobbies and vice versa. I've seen male engineers write about waltzing or painting, and I've seen artsy women write about motorcycles, fencing, and black-belt level karate.

List any hobbies or activities that present a dichotomy or could be considered atypical for your gender or type:

_____

_____

_____

_____

_____

_____

Some traditional extracurricular activities are actually more important than they appear on the surface. Finding the right angle is important. For example, I asked Ryan if he had ever done anything like save a person's life. He looked at me like I was crazy, but then went on to say, "Well, when I was on ski patrol…"

List any lifesaving or safety-related activities that may generate a good story.

_____

_____

_____

_____

_____

_____

On the other hand, you may have undertaken activities where you didn't realize at the time the influence you had. Personally, through work I had done for a U.S. congressman before going to business school, I helped release a prisoner of the former Soviet Union. I only realized this was essay-worthy while reading a novel about an imprisoned man in czarist Russia.

List activities where you may have had an influence beyond yourself.

_____

_____

_____

_____

_____

_____

WAYS TO FILL IN GAPS

If nothing comes to light from these ideas, take a look at the courses in your own community. I did a quick Internet search of courses that I could take if I wanted to do something different and challenge myself to do something I had never done before. I found the following courses in under 10 minutes:

✦ Fire Arts Performance
✦ Glass Blowing
✦ Neon Light Design
✦ Trapeze Arts
✦ Sign Language
✦ Screenwriting
✦ Taiko Drumming
✦ Ukulele

See if you can do something different just for the heck of it and how it gets you out of your comfort zone. I would have a hard time at fire arts, but could probably learn a lot about myself. Do some searching. What do you find?

_____

_____

_____

_____

_____

APPLICANT PROFILE

Jason decided to be more than just a member of Engineers Without Borders and ended up taking on increasing responsibilities. He ultimately ran the group's regional conference and then was elected president of one of the organization's more robust chapters.

While he was talented at engineering, he had not, up to that point, been very talented at organizing and speaking in public. So, he used the group as a platform to develop himself while helping develop infrastructure projects for those who needed them most. Jason is attending Duke's Fuqua MBA program.

COMMUNITY ACTIVITIES: GIVING BACK

In the exercises on the previous four pages, you may have included some of your community activities, such as working with a traditional group like Rebuilding Together (Habitat for Humanity), raising money for cancer research, going on a mission to do relief work in another country, or getting involved in Boys & Girls Clubs. The opportunities are endless. Many students have laid plans and even launched their own non-profits and social enterprises, admittedly with mixed results.

These days, you really *do* have to have some community service included in your application. But you don't have to start your own Nobel Peace Prize-winning charity. See if you can combine something you already like doing – say running marathons – and don't just raise money, but go out and put together a whole team of fundraisers.

Nobel Peace Prize Winner,
the Dalai Lama

What communities are you involved in? What does "community" mean to you?

_____

_____

_____

_____

_____

_____

List areas where you can marry your interests with community service.

_____

_____

_____

_____

_____

_____

APPLICANT PROFILE

Marta had very little, if any, work experience in an office other than a summer job in a law firm before her final year of university. After graduation, she spent two years teaching English in Asia. And that's the sum total of her work resume. So, we mined her undergraduate experience for instances of leadership potential.

We found a great example in her having produced a weekly comedy theater group. Naturally humble, Marta didn't recognize just how important she was to the troupe. She was booking agent, accountant, set manager, venue negotiator, babysitter for the "creatives," and seeker of any number of weird props, such as hula hoops. She helped put on 30 shows, brought the budget in line, and learned how to deal with craziness under tight deadlines, all culminating in a series of sell-out performances that put the troupe's name back on the map. Marta hopes to go into film production and will be attending NYU Stern in a joint MBA/MFA in film.

Admissions committee members are unanimous in wanting to see the genuine person behind the resume, GPA, and work experience. They do want you to delve into the depths of what makes you tick, but it doesn't necessarily mean you have to reveal family secrets. It does mean doing the work to get to the honest part, which entails answering tough questions. Those questions are daunting because they ask what makes *you* tick,

SELF-EXPLORATION OR EXCAVATION?

not your parents, college roommates, or cube-mate. You'll have to peel away the layers of your public persona to understand your strengths and weaknesses.

This isn't a process that you can do solo. You may have to talk to close friends, family, and former colleagues because sometimes we can't be objective about ourselves. Ask them to help you explore your patterns — the effective ones and the ones that need work.

> *You may have to talk to close friends, family, and former colleagues because sometimes we can't be objective about ourselves.*

You'll have to stand proud (but not boastful) of your successes and own up to your screw ups. It's a process from which most of us shy away; we don't really want to know the deep dark secrets and we may fear reaching too high. We are also afraid we won't like what we see when we look closely and are not sure we can take the rejection if we throw ourselves open for judgment.

It's a risk. But the reward at the end of the process is twofold: you'll know yourself better and be stronger for it, and you will have put together the best application to graduate school that you can. Only then will you feel you have done the best you can do to make your dreams come true.

CHAPTER 5: THE ESSAYS

Business schools want to get to know the real YOU. One of the first ways admissions committees look at the window to your soul is through your answers to the questions in the essay section. Although writing these essays can be overwhelming for some, especially for those who prefer working with numbers instead of words, it is a wonderful excuse for reflecting on your career goals, worthy qualities, and life experiences.

Before you even start writing, think about who you are as a person and the events in your life that have shaped you. **This is not something that can be done in a day or even a week**. It's a longer-term process and requires time between your insights. If you do it too fast, you may end up with answers that are great sound-bytes but convince no one.

Ultimately, you want to answer the million-dollar questions:

- ❖ Why you?
- ❖ Why the MBA?
- ❖ Why now?

The following exercises are intended to help you think about these questions and ruminate on all the points that come together to make you YOU.

There are no right or wrong answers to the prompts on the pages that follow. And remember, this is just for you to get your story right – you have to let your mind go a little crazy to come up with the answer that works for you. I feel like I have done my best job as an admissions coach when students look at their essays after we've done the very hard work and say, "Yes, everything about me in this essay is true. I had no idea my story was so interesting!"

> *...you have to let your mind go a little crazy to come up with the answer that works for you.*

You will also find that working through these exercises will help as you talk to people in informational interviews or conversations and eventually, in actual admissions interviews. Doing the work will help you get your authentic, genuine story out there. It's scary at first but a risk well worth taking.

So...let's get started.

This chapter is divided into four parts that explore the key aspects of your personality that the essay prompts are designed to elicit.

1. CHARACTER
2. INFLUENCE
3. LEADERSHIP
4. TEAMWORK

You don't have to answer all the questions on the following pages.

Questions are phrased in different ways so that you can find the ones that resonate with you. You will find if you answer all the questions, you may repeat themes — and that's fine. We're looking to trigger memories of events, ideas, or challenges that have made you grow up into the person you are today.

Business school applications will rarely come out and ask you any of these questions, but they are a first step to getting to know yourself, and that is critical to answering questions, including one of the most challenging questions of all time: Stanford GSB's "What is most important to you and why?" Even if you don't apply to Stanford, you will find that going through the process to answer some of the less challenging questions below might help you answer some of the broad questions that get at the heart of who you are and what makes you tick.

CHARACTER

The *character* section delves into who you are deep down inside. All the questions in a business school application are there to figure out what kind of person you are and how well you know yourself. These questions are also trying to figure out if you will be an interesting addition to the business school community.

Muhammad Ali, 1967

A. **DECISIONS**

1. Why did you choose the college you went to?

_____

_____

_____

_____

2. If you had all the money in the world, would you have gone to the same place? Why or why not?

_____

_____

_____

_____

_____

3. Why did you take the electives you took outside of your major?

_____

_____

_____

_____

_____

4. What job did you turn down when you got out of college? Why?

_____

_____

_____

_____

5. If you could start all over and work in any industry, what would it be? Why?

_____

_____

_____

_____

6. Where would you live in five years if family or money were not issues? Why?

_____

_____

_____

_____

7. If you had to do a joint-degree program, what would you choose? Why?

   a. _____

   b. _____

_____

_____

_____

_____

_____

_____

8. What are some of the most challenging choices you have had to make in your life so far?

_____

_____

_____

_____

_____

_____

B. **MOTIVATIONS**

1. What gives you energy? How?

_____

_____

_____

_____

_____

_____

2. What do you need to be committed to a process or an idea?

_____

_____

_____

_____

_____

_____

3. When have you surprised yourself?

_____

_____

_____

_____

_____

_____

4. What inspires you?

_____

_____

_____

_____

_____

_____

_____

_____

_____

5. Please write your definition of success.

_____

_____

_____

_____

_____

Fill in the blank:

I feel successful at work when

_____

_____

_____

_____

_____

I feel successful in my personal life when

_____

_____

_____

_____

_____

C. **ATTITUDES**

1. Would you call yourself optimistic? Why or why not?

_____

_____

_____

_____

_____

_____

_____

2. Describe a situation where you felt optimistic about the outcome. How did it influence those around you?

_____

_____

_____

_____

_____

_____

_____

3. Give an example of when you had to have an open mind.

_____

_____

_____

_____

_____

_____

_____

4. Define fun.

_____

_____

_____

_____

_____

_____

5. How do you present yourself when you feel passionate about something? Describe an example here.

_____

_____

_____

_____

_____

_____

6. If you get resistance, what do you do?

☐ Stamp your feet
☐ Stew
☐ Seethe
☐ Shut down
☐ Make it humorous
☐ Be reasonable
☐ Cajole, wheedle, nag, charm
☐ Be patient (the universe will do its magic)
☐ Give them facts
☐ Follow up

Give an example of a time when you found resistance to something about which you were passionate. Describe your actions.

_____

_____

_____

_____

_____

D. **ASPIRATIONS**

1. If there were no such thing as business school, what would you do?

_____

_____

_____

_____

_____

2. What have you always dreamed of doing?

_____

_____

_____

_____

_____

_____

_____

_____

_____

3. Would you consider yourself enterprising? How?

_____

_____

_____

_____

_____

_____

4. What have you NOT done that you wish you had done?

_____

_____

_____

_____

_____

_____

5. If you could change the world, how would you do it?

_____

_____

_____

_____

_____

_____

_____

_____

E. CREATIVITY

1. How do you demonstrate creativity in your day-to-day life?

_____

_____

_____

_____

_____

2. Have you ever done anything that was considered new or innovative? If so, explain.

_____

_____

_____

_____

_____

_____

_____

_____

INFLUENCE

This section covers both the influence others have on you and your own influence on others. The first exercise on people who influence you is not just about role models, but about the ideas and behaviors these people have taught you. In MBA applications, every so often you see questions about who you admire most – UC Berkeley's Haas School of Business used to have a question about sharing a meal with an admired person, and Indiana's Kelley School of Business had a question asking with whom you would choose to travel on a very long, cross-country road trip. The answers to those questions should include personal characteristics and attitudes of those who have inspired your path. And admissions committee members also want to know what you've learned from those people.

Oprah Winfrey, 2004

A. **INFLUENCERS**

✎ EXERCISE

This first exercise asks not only who influenced you, but who taught you the most.

Name people who have influenced you.

1. _____

2. _____

3. _____

4. _____

5. _____

6. _____

Don't just limit it to six, go on if you need to.

_____

_____

_____

_____

_____

_____

In the table below, next to each person's name, write down what you learned from him or her.

> For example:
> > Music teacher: *patience*
> > Mentor: *confidence*

Then, write down a specific circumstance where he or she demonstrated this characteristic or the circumstances where he or she taught you this lesson. I've given you some examples from my own life to get you started.

Teacher/Influencer	What	Takeaway
Pat S.	Re-taught me to read when I was an adult	Focus Patience
Ex-Boss, E.	Taught me how to write copy fast	Confidence Diplomacy
Sister	Makes me laugh	Humor Compassion
Ex-Boss, R.	He didn't support me	I cannot force peoples' actions

Teacher/Influencer	What	Takeaway

The previous exercise should help you figure out how you applied what you have learned as you've grown in your job and life. You'll want to incorporate your learning into the broader essays, particularly those that ask how you came to be the person you are today. For example, Columbia Business School asks you to write about a life experience that has shaped you. Later, after you do some of the rest of these exercises, you can try to write a story like the one that follows in the shaded box.

EXAMPLE

Linda's mentor (and manager at the time) led by example. When her company was going through layoffs, her manager was straight with everyone and told staff members the bad news in an honest way but also stayed optimistic. He kept everyone's spirits up, despite the craziness and uncertainty of downsizing. His cheerful, open demeanor kept everyone as productive as possible.

RELEVANCE

Linda modeled this manager's behavior when she was leading a team that was under pressure. She actively reached out to employees on her team to let them know what was going on and kept morale up. This benefitted her relationship with subordinates and other team members.

 **EXERCISES**

Who are your favorite people? Why?

_____

_____

_____

_____

_____

_____

What do you like about your friends?

_____

_____

_____

_____

_____

_____

What have you learned from a student or a mentee?

_____

_____

_____

_____

_____

_____

If

by Rudyard Kipling (1895)

If you can keep your head when all about you
Are losing theirs and blaming it on you,
If you can trust yourself when all men doubt you,
But make allowance for their doubting too;
If you can wait and not be tired by waiting,
Or, being lied about, don't deal in lies,
Or, being hated, don't give way to hating,
And yet don't look too good, nor talk too wise:

If you can dream - and not make dreams your master;
If you can think - and not make thoughts your aim;
If you can meet with Triumph and Disaster
And treat those two imposters just the same;
If you can bear to hear the truth you've spoken
Twisted by knaves to make a trap for fools,
Or watch the things you gave your life to broken,
And stoop and build 'em up with wornout tools:

If you can make one heap of all your winnings
And risk it on one turn of pitch-and-toss,
And lose, and start again at your beginnings
And never breathe a word about your loss;
If you can force your heart and nerve and sinew
To serve your turn long after they are gone,
And so hold on when there is nothing in you
Except the Will which says to them: 'Hold on!'

If you can talk with crowds and keep your virtue,
Or walk with Kings - nor lose the common touch,
If neither foes nor loving friends can hurt you,
If all men count with you, but none too much;
If you can fill the unforgiving minute
With sixty seconds' worth of distance run,
Yours is the Earth and everything that's in it,
And - which is more - you'll be a Man my son!

YOUR INFLUENCE: DEMONSTRATION OF KEY STRENGTHS

This section may be particularly useful to review as you prepare for interviews. You may find it helpful to use some of the stories you come up with in this section as a primer for your recommenders.

A. DEMONSTRATION OF FLEXIBILITY, POISE, AND/OR MATURITY

Admissions officers know you are human and that you are not Superman. However, even the most humble people need to discuss their key strengths in the application. In this section, you'll be asked questions that highlight strengths that you might not have even known were important.

Note that you won't have demonstrated these strengths in every situation you've ever faced. In one instance you may have shown great courage, and another, well, it didn't work out so well. We're just trying to isolate incidents of excellence — in any aspect of your life — as they are usually part of a larger pattern.

1. Have you ever kept calm while everyone around you wasn't? When? How? What happened?

_____

_____

_____

_____

_____

_____

_____

_____

_____

2. Have you ever successfully planned out a project well in advance, replete with back-up options in case something went wrong? Describe it.

_____

_____

_____

_____

_____

_____

3. Have you ever had to think fast on your feet as circumstances changed? When?

_____

_____

_____

_____

_____

_____

4. Have you ever persisted in the face of challenges and/or unexpected difficulties? When? What did you learn?

_____

_____

_____

_____

_____

_____

5. Give an example where you had to deal with ambiguity at work.

_____

_____

_____

_____

_____

_____

B. THE SKILL OF PERSUASION

Not everyone is an extrovert or great salesperson. However, nearly everyone has been able to convince someone of something and has used his or her own personal style to do it.

These exercises are designed to help you figure out when you may have prevailed in your argument, and even changed someone's mind. You will probably find some form of these questions in the formal essays. For example, MIT Sloan School of Management has asked, "Please describe a time when you convinced an individual or group to accept one of your ideas." Having good solid answers to these types of questions can help you in an interview setting, particularly the behavioral-style interview.

1. Have you ever sold an idea to a group? If so, how?

_____

_____

_____

_____

_____

_____

2. Have you ever convinced anyone to change his or her mind or overcome someone's objections? Even if it didn't work 100%? How did you do it?

_____

_____

_____

_____

_____

3. Have you ever had to compromise to reach an agreement? If so, give an example.

_____

_____

_____

_____

_____

4. Have you ever played the diplomat? Under what circumstance?

_____

_____

_____

_____

5. Have you ever taught a class? What did you learn about yourself after it was over?

_____

_____

_____

_____

C. **MASTERY**

I have found that students often underestimate their talents, especially when they are writing about themselves in the essays. They often say to me, "Oh, lots of people do that," when talking about some achievement that they consider fairly mundane. The truth is, some of these seemingly routine behaviors show up in the rest of your life and turn into some terrific attributes in business and business school.

EXERCISES

Take a look at the examples below to see how being good at something carries over to all parts of your life.

<u>AT HOME</u>:

> **Examples:**

Q.   What are you good at?
A.   *Being a good brother or sister.*

Q.   Name a characteristic that represents being a good sibling.
A.   *Responsibility.*

Q.   Where else did you use the characteristic?
      (For example, how do you show responsibility at work or in outside activities/ventures?)
A.   *1. Volunteering to lead a work task force*
      2. Organizing a fundraiser
      3. Being the one to get things done when the "buck stops"

What are you good at?

_____

_____

_____

_____

_____

_____

_____

Name a characteristic that represents what you're good at:

_____

How did you show _____ (fill in the blank with characteristic) at work or in outside activities/ventures?

1. _____

_____

_____

2. _____

_____

_____

3. _____

_____

_____

DURING UNDERGRADUATE DAYS:

☐ **Examples:**

Q.   What were you good at?
A.   *Having many friends and contacts because I had decent social skills and valued others' contributions.*

Q.   Where else have you used your social skills in professional relationships?
A.   *1. Sales skills in pitching business*
       2. Representing the group at a firm-wide meeting/event
       3. Acted as a broker/mediator/problem solver

Make a list of other things you might have been good at, even things that you think may not be a big deal. For example, Jeremy has hardly ever paid full price for anything. As a result, he is always asked to lead negotiating teams, and often ends up with surprisingly successful results.

_____

_____

_____

_____

_____

_____

_____

_____

_____

_____

_____

OUTSIDE OF WORK:

⬜ **Examples:**

Q: What are you good at?
A: 1. *Playing group sports*
         ✦ Doing well on teams, being an active team member, leader,
           follower

    2. *Enjoying individual sports; for example: weightlifting,
        long-distance running*
         ✦ Goal setting, not simply for the sake of goals, but to really
           accomplish something that makes a difference to you

    3. *Coaching a team*
         ✦ Teaching, mentoring, training

    4. *Music*
         ✦ Being creative, having inspiration, able to compose,
           orchestrate

    5. *Telling jokes*
         ✦ Making people feel comfortable, presenting, timing delivery of
           information

    6. *Tutoring*
         ✦ Teaching, inspiring, training, mentoring, having patience, having
           faith in someone

    7. *Building or making things*
         ✦ Structuring things, solving problems, designing solutions

    8. *Cooking*
         ✦ Creating, experimenting, bringing things and people together

A VARIATION

I've used a variation of the mastery exercises with students, which yields surprising results. We start with: *What do you do well that you wouldn't mind doing badly?*

I've gotten great answers, including "milk a cow." Another that I find refreshingly honest is "worry" or "obsess over small things." One aspiring student wrote, "navigating large bureaucracies." You can see the frustration, yet pride in working with large organizations and having actual successes. The candidate used that point in building an argument that he was able to get things done under a wide variety of circumstances.

What do you do well that you wouldn't mind doing badly?

_____

_____

And for a variation on a variation, I also ask students to complete this sentence:

I wish I could be better at

_____

_____

This question is important in your work life as well as your application process. You can always get better. In annual reviews, my bosses always asked me to put together a development plan, which might mean getting better at a technical task (for example, risk management) or learning ways to make my team more cohesive. In business school, you will constantly find things you wish you could be better at: financial modeling, presenting in public, or critical thinking, to name a few. Almost every school application asks you why you want the MBA and asks you to talk intelligently about your gaps. Some explicitly ask such a question. For example, Georgetown asks, "What areas do you wish to develop in order to become a more effective leader?"

This leads us to the next section, a specific focus on leadership.

LEADERSHIP

U.S. President Abraham Lincoln, 1860

Your biggest goal in the MBA admissions process is to demonstrate leadership. Business schools may have leadership classes, workshops, or what Stanford calls "Leadership Labs," but the schools are not working with blank slates. Admissions committees want to see candidates with great leadership *potential*. This potential can be demonstrated through a record of traditional leadership activities, such as president of your undergraduate student body or manager of your unit at work. We covered titled (and non-titled) positions of leadership in Chapter 3: Work Experience, and Chapter 4: Extracurricular Activities. This chapter goes a bit further. It tries to get you to think and write about times you've shown leadership when you didn't have a title, or when you used your natural traits to show what kind of leader you could be.

"Leadership encompasses much more than managing people," wrote Rosemaria Martinelli, former director of Admissions at the University of Chicago Booth School of Business.[1] Business schools now equate leadership with influence, or the ability to motivate others toward a shared goal. Stanford Graduate School of Business' recommendation form includes a "Leadership Behavior Grid" with traits such as initiative, influence and collaboration, developing others, and trustworthiness. Dartmouth's Tuck School of Business defines leadership as "the ability to inspire others to strive and enable them to accomplish great things."[2]

> *Your biggest goal in the MBA admissions process is to demonstrate leadership.*

Leadership can mean anything from running a classroom to being the idea person in your work team, from standing up for an unpopular position to organizing a clothing drive. In a nutshell, leadership is about finding the passion inside you and acting on it.

[1] http://blogs.chicagobooth.edu/n/blogs/blog.aspx?nav=main&webtag=RoseReport&entry=28
[2] http://www.tuck.dartmouth.edu/recruiting/connect_with_students/leadership.html

RELEVANT LINKS

🖰   Stanford Business School Leadership Labs:

http://www.gsb.stanford.edu/cldr/teaching/leadershiplabs.html

🖰   Leadership Behavior Grid:

http://www.gsb.stanford.edu/mba/admission/2012_entry_LBGrid_LOR.pdf

EMOTIONAL IQ

Business schools are actively searching for students with high emotional intelligence. In a seminal 1998 *Harvard Business Review* article, "What Makes a Leader,"[3] Daniel Goleman attempted to answer the question with specific attributes of effective leaders. Goleman, who popularized the concept of emotional intelligence with his book of the same name, wrote in the HBR article: "It's not that IQ and technical skills are irrelevant....They do matter, but mainly as 'threshold capabilities.' But...emotional intelligence is the *sine qua non* of leadership."

Goleman's model of emotional intelligence has dramatically improved the global discussion of leadership. In his research of nearly 200 large, global companies, Goleman found that

> *while the qualities traditionally associated with leadership – such as intelligence, toughness, determination, and vision – are required for success, they are insufficient. **Truly effective leaders are also distinguished by a high degree of emotional intelligence, which includes self-awareness, self-regulation, motivation, empathy, and social skill.***

[3] Goleman, Daniel, "What Makes a Leader," Harvard Business Review, Harvard Business Review (1998) Volume: 76, Issue: 6, Pages: 93-102

🖰   Available without subscription on the web at:
https://www.mercy.edu/faculty/Georgas/inbs640/files/WhatMakesaLeader.pdf

Characteristic	How it Plays Out at Work According to Daniel Goleman
Self-Awareness	Honest with themselves and others. Goleman: *People who have a high degree of self-awareness recognize how their feelings affect them, other people, and their job performance.*
Self-Regulation	In control of feelings and impulses. Goleman: *Comfort with ambiguity and change, and integrity – an ability to say no to impulsive urges.*
Motivation	Passion for work itself. Goleman: *They are forever raising the performance bar, and they like to keep score. Remain optimistic even when the score is against them.*
Empathy	Intuitive, not mushy. Goleman: *Thoughtful consideration of others' feelings – along with other factors – in making decisions.*
Social Skill	People and team focused. Goleman: *Socially skilled people work according to the assumption that nothing important gets done alone.*

Source, Harvard Business Review, 1998, "Goleman, What Makes a Leader"

These five components of emotional intelligence – self-awareness, self-regulation, motivation, empathy, and social skill – comprise a useful framework for writing admissions essays. Any question prompt that begins with "Tell us about a time when…" is looking for you to demonstrate your leadership through emotional intelligence.

The exercises on the following pages discusses Goleman's five components of leadership. Each component has an example prompting you to think about where you might have demonstrated emotional intelligence. A candidate need not show all five of these components, but should be able to demonstrate a healthy number of these characteristics in his or her application.

A. SELF-AWARENESS

Business schools want their students to know who they are and to understand their own foibles. They recognize that a 27-year-old still has a lot to learn but is an adult who knows who she is inside and the effect she has on others.

> *Business schools recognize that a 27-year-old still has a lot to learn but is an adult who knows who she is inside and the effect she has on others.*

They also are looking for candidates who know why they do what they do. If you turned down a job with a big salary because you learned the company advocated selling tobacco to minors, explain that the organization did not fit with your ethics or goals. If you knew the answer to a question at an important meeting but knew you weren't expected to say anything in front of the CEO and his biggest investor, explain why you chose to stay quiet. The point is to prove you know who you are and make appropriate decisions.

> **APPLICANT PROFILE**
>
> Bob was very talented and rose rapidly through his career straight out of Wharton. He was often sought out by senior managers because they found his self-deprecating sense of humor refreshing. He was confident of his abilities, but not overconfident. When faced with exhausting hours on an investment banking deal, he handled the pressure in stride and was realistic about the part he could play. He knew his human boundaries.

Can you describe an example where you had to know your own limits? Or where you had to know what effect you had on others?

_____

_____

_____

_____

B. **SELF-REGULATION**

Goleman identifies "comfort with ambiguity" and "openness to change" as hallmarks of the self-regulation component of emotional intelligence. Business life is filled with unpredictable events. The leaders who will excel are the ones who will be able to handle change – not in a detached way, but realistically. Stuff happens. Sometimes it is good for the bottom line, sometimes not. And sometimes it's just not clear.

Comfort with ambiguity means not freaking out when the company might be taken over, or there are layoffs, or a big client left for a competitor.

Self-regulation is about putting your emotions on hold. It's about handling things diplomatically and without blame when a co-worker lets you down. Comfort with ambiguity means not freaking out when the company might be taken over, or there are layoffs, or a big client left for a competitor.

APPLICANT PROFILE

Sunita doesn't let her ego get in the way. Even though she works in the retail industry amidst lots of drama, she manages to stay cool. When her presence on a consulting project was criticized by a senior client executive, she figured out a way to do great work and eventually turn this adversary into her biggest supporter. Sunita bravely sought a one-on-one meeting with the client executive, only to find that the client felt shunted aside. The client wanted to participate in the process, specifically wanting to help the consulting team evaluate their decisions. From then on, the client executive became an integral member of the team and Sunita's biggest champion. Sunita will be attending the Duke Fuqua School of Business full-time MBA program.

Provide an example where you had to stay cool when your emotions told you to do something else:

_____

_____

_____

_____

_____

_____

C. **MOTIVATION**

Most MBA candidates are highly motivated; anyone who has gone through the GMAT ordeal has a strong drive to achieve. Goleman says that motivation also encompasses "optimism, even in the face of failure." Motivation complements the essay questions that ask you to describe how you learned from a mistake or failure; not only does a strong leader stay motivated when things aren't going his way, he is also open to learning from his mistakes. (See p. 106, "Resiliency.")

> *Highly motivated people are not afraid to measure their success and are not afraid to keep trying.*

Many entrepreneurs are deeply motivated, especially considering all the people they may face who say it cannot be done. Outside of the startup world, we've all seen people who are motivated to run races, meet goals, and outshine the competition, especially when they have a fire in their belly. Highly motivated people are not afraid to measure their success and are not afraid to keep trying. Motivated individuals set the bar high, and self-aware, motivated individuals set it high enough so it presents a significant challenge while not being impossible.

APPLICANT PROFILE

Lee has a passion for work that goes beyond money and status. He co-founded a social-networking site that has grown from two founders and no members to a staff of 10 and two million members. He was offered the chance to work for a traditional company but turned it down because he is passionate about his venture and believes more than anything that it will thrive. He loves building things and is energized by the growth of the community he's nurtured. Lee was admitted to his first-choice MBA program but turned it down to stay on top of his business. At this point, he doesn't look back.

Can you remember a time when you were unusually motivated in a business setting? If so, explain.

_____

_____

_____

_____

_____

_____

_____

_____

D. EMPATHY

Goleman makes clear that empathy isn't about people-pleasing. Rather, he says, it's about "thoughtfully considering employees' feelings – along with other factors – in the process of making intelligent decisions." This could show itself as cross-cultural sensitivity or outstanding service to clients and customers. And for managers, empathy will show up as expertise in building and retaining talent.

Professionals with clear-headed empathy toward their teammates add to the productivity of the entire group. These types engender trust and likely have a knack for smoothing things out among squabbling teammates. They may be the ones who encourage a teammate who is struggling or may simply be terrific listeners.

Empathetic professionals are the ones who people turn to in times of uncertainty, say, in the case of a company merger or rocky economic patch. These sometimes unsung heroes are the glue that keeps organizations going when the going gets rough.

> *Professionals with clear-headed empathy toward their teammates add to the productivity of the entire group.*

APPLICANT PROFILE

Mike was an officer in the U.S. Army and had to rally his platoon for one last training exercise that required rescuing a downed helicopter pilot. While they were all exhausted, Mike noticed that one member of his team appeared especially disheartened. He called this particular infantryman aside and asked what was up. The soldier was sure he would fail, and didn't feel he understood how he could succeed in this exercise. Mike encouraged the infantryman to talk about what he felt he could do well. Mike then planned a strategy where each team member, including the less confident one, played to his strengths. The team passed the training exercise the following day with flying colors. Mike is now attending MIT Sloan School of Management.

Can you give an example of a time or situation in which you have shown compassionate leadership? Or been able to smooth things out between people in an organization? Or been able to use listening skills to improve your decision-making ability?

_____

_____

_____

_____

_____

_____

_____

_____

_____

_____

_____

E. **SOCIAL SKILL**

Social skill shows itself as "a knack for building rapport," and "effectiveness in leading change." The phrase "social skill" can sometimes be misinterpreted, implying that an individual is popular or merely a smooth operator. Social skill shows itself in diplomacy, in giving and receiving feedback, and in managing teams. The professional with social skill knows how to make things work together better. Social skill can also help get things done. This trait is one of the most important differences between the leader and the manager.

> *Social skill can also help get things done. This trait is one of the most important differences between the leader and the manager.*

Can you recall a time when you used your social skills to benefit a larger goal?

_____

_____

_____

_____

_____

_____

_____

MANAGING YOURSELF THROUGH CHANGE AND DISAPPOINTMENT

Transformation makes great essay copy. It also makes terrific screenplay copy, and, like the hero's journey, is a tried-and-true theme. Think of a play or movie. The character has one way of looking at the world in the beginning, learns something surprising, and then looks at the world differently. This is a classic character arc and represents growth.

Sam's character in *Avatar* was a narrow-minded paraplegic at the beginning of the film but was literally transformed by the end of the film. The change and self-awareness can also develop more subtly and surprisingly. Morgan Freeman's character in *The Shawshank Redemption* appears to be a friendly but distant narrator throughout much of the film. But by the end, when he realizes what Tim Robbins has been doing all along, he realizes something about himself that he didn't know before: that he is not so disengaged after all. Transformation can also come from within. In the very last scene of *The Social Network*, even the fictional Mark Zuckerberg appears different – more mature, perhaps?

In the following exercises we will look for times when you changed, or even just felt a subtle but powerful shift.

✎ EXERCISES

1. When did you change your mind about something important? Why?

   _____

   _____

   _____

   _____

   _____

   _____

   _____

   _____

2. Have you ever surprised yourself by changing your point of view? Why were you surprised? What forced the switch?

   _____

   _____

   _____

   _____

   _____

   _____

   _____

   _____

3. Think of a time when you found yourself changed from the inside. What caused the change? Was it an external force that catalyzed something that was already in motion?

_____

_____

_____

_____

_____

_____

_____

_____

_____

Was the change bad? (Of course not!) What did you learn from the change or what did you learn from the process?

_____

_____

_____

_____

_____

_____

_____

_____

_____

_____

_____

APPLICANT PROFILE

Despite being based in Boston, Amy was sent to work on a deal in Brazil for what was supposed to be two weeks, but turned out to be four months. It was a very lonely experience, and she missed going home for Easter, a very big deal in her family. The project in Sao Paolo seemed cursed and she had to handle a number of issues on her own. In several instances, she had to make some decisions without any input from senior management.

After finishing the project, she wished she could get back those four months of her life. But she felt something was different; she had grown in some way. She was more confident that she could handle herself in unsupported situations and not worry so much about ambiguity in the future. Though she knows everything isn't going to go the way she wants all the time, she feels like she has undergone a rite of passage and is stronger for it. Amy is attending the University of Chicago's Booth School of Business.

RESILIENCY

Some business school applications come right out and ask about times when you've made a mistake or times when you've failed or been disappointed. There's a significant question behind the question, sometimes stated explicitly with the words: "What have you learned from...?" Everyone moans and cries about not knowing how to talk about their failures.

MICHAEL JORDAN'S LAST WORD ON FAILURE

 Michael Jordan didn't even make the varsity team in high school after attending a summer basketball camp. But he learned from having his mistakes corrected and repeating those corrections over and over. He got better – much better – by continually improving the weakest part of his game. You can watch his inspirational message in a powerful Nike ad on YouTube:

> *I've missed more than 9,000 shots in my career.*
> *I've lost almost 300 games.*
> *Twenty-six times I've been trusted to take the game-winning shot.*
> *And missed.*
> *I've failed over and over and over again in my life.*
> *And that is why*
> *I succeed.*

Here's the deal: the story is NOT about the failure. It's about your learning and recovery. It's about growth – and the end result doesn't always have to be a brilliant success.

🖱 Source: Michael Jordan "Failure" commercial
http://youtu.be/45mMioJ5szc

 **EXERCISES**

The question about failure probably requires the most self-awareness of any question in an application. Getting there requires a little digging, so see what you can come up with in your responses to the questions below.

1. What is the biggest thing that happened to you that was totally outside your control?

   _____

   _____

   _____

   _____

   _____

2. How did you react? Did you end up "slaying a dragon"? Can you turn this into a hero's journey story? Can you make a story about how this showed leadership?

   _____

   _____

   _____

   _____

   _____

   _____

   _____

   _____

   _____

3. What has been your biggest obstacle up to this point?

   _____

   _____

   _____

   _____

4. Have you ever had to take responsibility for a group failure? What did it feel like?

   _____

   _____

   _____

5. Have you ever been misinterpreted by senior management? What did you do to fix the misunderstanding?

   _____

   _____

   _____

   _____

6. What do you do when someone asks you a question and you don't know the answer?

   _____

   _____

   _____

   _____

   _____

7. How do you respond when someone tells you that you've made a mistake?

_____

_____

_____

8. Think of a time when you were in a tight spot, preferably professionally. How did you get out of it? What did this experience teach you?

_____

_____

_____

_____

_____

_____

_____

_____

RISK MANAGEMENT

Every effort requires a calculated risk: walking out the door, getting on an airplane, climbing Mount Everest. You will learn about risk management in finance class, but you will also learn about taking risks in the business school environment – because if you don't take risks, you'll never learn.

When I was at Harvard Business School, one of the sections had T-shirts made up with the (now-tired) expression, "No Guts, No Glory." The University of Chicago Booth School of Business used to have an application question that began with the statement: "Chicago Booth is a place that challenges its students to stretch and take risks that they might not take elsewhere." In the next set of exercises, think about risks while also considering risk management. Were your risks calculated risks, or just crazy?

✎ EXERCISES

1. What is your personal definition of risky?

   _____

   _____

   _____

   _____

2. Have you ever gone outside your comfort zone? What did it feel like? What did you learn?

   _____

   _____

   _____

   _____

   _____

   _____

3. What's the most courageous thing you've ever done?

   _____

   _____

   _____

   _____

   _____

   _____

   _____

   _____

4. What is the most courageous thing you wish you could do?

_____

_____

_____

_____

_____

_____

_____

5. Have you ever pushed yourself beyond your own expected limits? What did it feel like?

_____

_____

_____

6. Have you ever taken a risk and failed? Did the world end? What did you learn? (see the "Resiliency" section, p. 106)

_____

_____

_____

_____

_____

_____

_____

_____

TEAMWORK

Teams are the heart and soul of the MBA experience because they reflect what goes on in business every day. People work in groups and on teams – and those teams make things happen. Even if they don't proclaim it incredibly loudly in their own marketing messages, business schools want to know how you work on a team. *Harvard Business Review* lists 755 articles and nearly 2,400 cases on teams and their dynamics. Some teams work well while others fail magnificently; many muddle along in between. This set of exercises helps you determine your potential role within a team, where you might need to grow as a team player, and how you can mine your team experience for great stories

Discovery Space Shuttle Team, October 2007

that demonstrate your leadership potential to MBA admissions officers. You don't have to answer every question, but I've included a variety so that if one question doesn't inspire you, another might.

✎ EXERCISES

1. Have you ever had to organize a group of people? How did it go?

   _____

   _____

   _____

   _____

   _____

2. How do you tend to contribute your ideas when in a group?

_____

_____

_____

_____

_____

_____

_____

3. How would you rate your listening ability? How could it be improved?

_____

_____

_____

_____

_____

_____

_____

4. Can you give an example where active listening helped your case?

_____

_____

_____

_____

_____

_____

_____

5. Where do you see yourself adding value:

   a. To your study group mates?

   _____

   _____

   _____

   b. To the school?

   _____

   _____

   _____

   c. To your classmates?

   _____

   _____

   _____

6. Have you ever hired anyone or had an influence in hiring someone? Was it successful?

   _____

   _____

7. If it was not so successful, how did you work with that person?

   _____

   _____

   _____

   _____

   _____

8. Have you ever fired anyone? How did it go?

_____

_____

_____

_____

_____

9. Have you ever had anyone report to you? What was it like?

_____

_____

_____

_____

_____

10. Have you ever mentored someone at work or outside of work? Who and how?

_____

_____

_____

_____

_____

_____

_____

11. When have you ever coordinated a project? How did it go?

_____

_____

_____

_____

12. Where do you think you add the most value on a project team?

_____

_____

_____

_____

13. What's the most successful project you have ever been a part of?

_____

_____

_____

_____

14. When have you mediated a dispute or solved a problem between team members? What worked? What didn't? What did you learn?

_____

_____

_____

_____

_____

_____

15. Was there ever a time when you ensured that a task was completed even though other group members were less focused than you? How did you achieve it?

_____

_____

_____

_____

_____

_____

_____

16. Have you ever been in a situation where politics overwhelmed the team? Did you learn anything about yourself? Could you have prevented things from getting off course? How would you have behaved differently?

_____

_____

_____

_____

_____

_____

_____

_____

_____

_____

_____

_____

17. Have you ever supported someone even when the crowd seemed against him or her? If yes, how? What was the outcome?

_____

_____

_____

_____

_____

_____

18. Have you ever hatched an idea with someone else? What was the chemistry between you? How did it work out?

_____

_____

_____

_____

_____

_____

_____

19. Have you ever invented anything? How did it happen? Who did you confer with and what was the dynamic?

_____

_____

_____

_____

_____

_____

20. In what kind of non-work teams have you been involved?

_____

_____

_____

_____

_____

_____

_____

_____

_____

_____

_____

FOLLOWERSHIP

Being part of a team also means understanding what it is to be a follower. As Professor Robert E. Kelley of Carnegie Mellon's Tepper School writes in his landmark 1988 *Harvard Business Review "In Praise of Followers,"*

> *What distinguishes an effective from an ineffective follower is enthusiastic, intelligent, and self-reliant participation – without star billing – in the pursuit of an organizational goal.*

Look at any sports team and you will see great followers. Do you know who Orlando Cabrera is? I didn't. He was the shortstop for the Boston Red Sox in 2004. Not voted the most valuable player, or the best hitter, Cabrera's excellent defensive efforts helped the Sox beat the New York Yankees to pull off the amazing come-from-behind win for the league championship and shut out the Cardinals 4-0 in the World Series.

✎ EXERCISES

1. When have you been a follower? What did it feel like?

   _____

   _____

   _____

   _____

   _____

   _____

2. What kind of impact did you have as a follower?

   _____

   _____

   _____

   _____

   _____

   _____

3. Think of a time when you were a reluctant follower. How would you have
   rated your leader? Could you have seen yourself switching roles?

   _____

   _____

   _____

   _____

   _____

   _____

GIVING AND RECEIVING FEEDBACK

This is a tough area for everyone, especially for emerging leaders. Many times we've been given feedback that is better classified as criticism. Even the term "constructive criticism" has the ring of, "Oh that color isn't quite right for you, have you considered…wearing a bag over your head?" But feedback is how we get better, and modern management thinking is trying to incorporate it into daily business life.

Business schools are working hard on developing people who know how to both give and receive feedback. Stanford's Graduate School of Business courses depend heavily on this dynamic — not only are students required to give feedback to their teammates, but they give feedback on how they give feedback!

Feedback is neutral. It is not criticism; it is information. The exercises below are about both positive and negative feedback. Business schools want you to recognize that both are necessary for great teamwork.

✎ EXERCISES

1. Have you ever given feedback on a colleague's work? How did it go? What could you have done better?

   _____

   _____

   _____

   _____

   _____

   _____

   _____

   _____

2. How could you have been more comfortable giving feedback?

_____

_____

_____

_____

_____

3. Have you ever received helpful feedback from a work or non-work peer? What worked? What didn't?

_____

_____

_____

_____

_____

_____

_____

4. Have you ever received positive feedback from someone you respected? How did you receive it? What did you do next?

_____

_____

_____

_____

_____

_____

_____

_____

5. Have you ever received negative feedback from someone you respected? How did you respond or improve the problem?

_____

_____

_____

_____

_____

_____

BIT OF ADVICE

Getting Feedback on Your Essays

Your application will be read by several members of a committee, each with differing points of view. Your support team wants to help you, and you should let them by taking into consideration their observations and suggestions.

So who are you going to ask for feedback? Here are some suggestions:

✦ Ex-college roommate
✦ Journalist
✦ Admissions consultant
✦ Husband/wife/girlfriend/boyfriend
✦ Current student or alumna of target school
✦ Really good writer or thinker
✦ Clear-thinking work colleague
✦ Others: _____

_____

_____

CHAPTER 6: RECOMMENDATION WRANGLING

Organizing and managing the recommendation process can be a challenge, especially if you are applying to a number of different schools. But it's a lot like managing a project at work: you've got to get buy-in from people who will be helping you and make sure they meet deadlines. You also want to choose the right recommender, and you want to be able to give him or her enough time to write the kind of recommendation that will help your overall application. Wrangling your recommender has an added benefit of teaching you firsthand how to use your influencing skills to get someone to write you a letter that adds value to your application.

125

CHOOSE CAREFULLY

Keep in mind that business schools want to accept honest, decent people. They expect you to choose recommenders who know you well and can write in-depth letters that convey both your strengths and weaknesses. Admissions committees want to see that your recommenders can confirm the qualities and information you've expressed to them in the other parts of your application.

They are also looking to see who's writing the letter and the kind of genuine relationship you two have formed. If you have a choice between Bill Gates, who is willing to write you a letter because your father is a friend of a friend, and your direct supervisor with whom you work day in and day out, choose your direct supervisor.

> *If you have a choice between Bill Gates, who is willing to write you a letter because your father is a friend of a friend, and your direct supervisor with whom you work day in and day out, choose your direct supervisor.*

The person writing you a letter of recommendation should know you personally and know you well. This kind of relationship will make the letter stronger and more persuasive, giving you more credibility with the admissions board. The recommender **must** be the one writing this letter — you should not be writing it for him or her, even if you do give suggestions and guidance on how to approach it. This is an ethical issue, and you want to be honest with the school from the start.

As for timing, you should probably give your recommenders a heads up **two to three months** in advance. Then sit down with them over coffee (or on the phone if you aren't in the same locale) and help them help you. On the following pages, you'll find some models for presenting solid stories for the letter writer.

EXERCISES

Put your potential recommenders in a list. For each individual, make sure you can answer *yes* for each item in the following checklist:

✓ Was a supervisor, not a peer* or direct report

✓ Is more senior in terms of life experience

✓ Will champion your cause

✓ Is able to rank you at the top among others in your peer group

✓ Will be able to tell stories rather than brush the surface

✓ Will not make you write the recommendation yourself

✓ Has time and is willing to talk over what you need him or her to say

Note: Stanford GSB asks for a peer review in addition to two supervisor reviews, but other than item number one, the rest hold true.

> *"What we are hoping for are brief recounts of specific situations and how you performed."*
>
> *– Dee Leopold*
> *HBS Admissions Director*

If a recommender does not meet all these requirements, see if you can come up with someone else who does. You really, really want someone who knows you and is willing to promote your case. Many business schools weigh equally the recommendations and the essays.

Almost every admissions director under the sun will tell you they want your recommender to give specific examples rather than just surface compliments. Harvard Business School's Dee Leopold says in her blog: "Many recommendations are well written and enthusiastic in their praise but essentially full of adjectives and short on actual examples of how your wonderful qualities play out in real life." She continues: "What we are hoping for are brief recounts of specific situations and how you performed."[4]

You can help your recommenders by giving them some written material with which to work. The following templates may help you remind your recommenders of specific instances worth mentioning as they answer the specific questions in their recommendation form.

[4] Admissions Director's Blog, Aug 24, 2009 http://www.hbs.edu/mba/admissions/blog-all.html

LEADERSHIP STORY TEMPLATE

Go back through the portion of your resume where you worked with your recommender.

For example, Jennifer's resume had the following bullet point:

- *Managed strategic planning and re-branding campaign for 15-year-old non-profit*

That is a tangible, measurable event and worth discussing in a recommendation. Even if Jennifer wrote about it as a hero's story within her essay package (see "The Hero's Model" p. 45), by definition, her point of view is different from that of her supervisor. It's a bit like a 360-degree review, only with two data points: Jennifer and her supervisor.

For the letter, Jennifer's recommender can use the same story, but should use a slightly different approach from that of the hero's journey. To help the recommender, put together bullet points or a short paragraph, using the following template to make sure it is all included.

Event:
Management of strategic planning and re-branding campaign

Impact:
Changed the organization from a staid, outdated "charity" to a modern, dynamic non-profit

Tangible, measurable results:
Raised profile of organization by getting favorable publicity in international press, increased donations by x%, and increased local recipient organizations by y%

Methodology:
Used for-profit strategic management tools, such as questioning the status quo and coming up with actionable ways to move the organization forward

Demonstrated leadership traits:
Organization, motivation, calm under pressure, ability to communicate at various levels of an organization

Now try it with a chosen bullet point from your resume:

Event:

_____

_____

Impact:

_____

_____

Tangible, measurable results:

_____

_____

_____

Methodology:

_____

_____

_____

Demonstrated leadership traits:

_____

_____

_____

_____

TEAMWORK CHARACTERISTIC TEMPLATE

The recommendation letter does not require that the writer discuss only your greatest accomplishments. He might also want to talk about your teamwork skills, many of which don't show up on your resume. If you have a specific teamwork story that you want your recommenders to recount, that makes their job easy. However, if you are just talking about a day-to-day trait such as being responsible, helpful, and industrious, try the model below.

Situation:

One of five members on emerging markets research team

Personal/professional qualities:

industrious, responsible, helpful, steps up, eye on the bottom line

Example*:*

Carried weight of a full senior team member as a junior team member (e.g., wrote monthly portfolio reports for investors, performed macroeconomic research), mentored and brought up to speed newer team members, got along with everyone (unusual in this industry), helped others meet their deadlines. For example, when team member Matthew was out of the country, candidate single-handedly put together a pitch for institutional business that brought in $X million in assets to the fund.

Situation:

_____

_____

Personal/professional qualities:

_____

_____

Example:

_____

_____

_____

_____

In putting together personal and professional qualities, don't forget to go back to the section in Chapter 5: Essays, on "Demonstration of Key Strengths", p. 85 and "Emotional Intelligence", p. 95, and make sure you include tangible examples!

As you prepare the package for your recommenders, in addition to the leadership story template or teamwork characteristic template, you might add or substitute a _professional growth_ or _interpersonal dynamic_ template.

WHY BUSINESS SCHOOL?

You definitely want to give your recommender a two-to-three sentence nugget on why you want to go to business school to reinforce what you've already discussed when you asked him or her to help you. If you've done the Career Progression Warm-up Exercise (p. 38) and the experiment in the section "How to Talk About Your Career Goals" (p. 47), you shouldn't have to struggle to come up with anything new.

See if you can articulate it here – just two or three sentences will do:

_____

_____

_____

_____

_____

_____

WEAKNESSES: THE ACHILLES' HEEL

Face it — no one wants to write about their weaknesses, and most people do a terrible job of it. You can relieve your recommenders of this odious duty by giving them real, sensible examples of areas where you know you need work or have already made some healthy changes.

Below are some examples to get you started on a (hopefully) short list of areas for development.

Sample Weakness	Sample Awareness or Action to Improve
Too quiet in group discussions	Starting to speak up more (give example), started going to Toastmasters for public speaking training
Avoids conflict	Give example of being able to talk through a solution when you disagreed with someone on your team
Not diplomatic; too opinionated	Took a workshop on giving and receiving feedback, resulting in a more mature presence on the team
Missed a number of important deadlines	Time management training, or example of new pattern of successful on-time delivery of projects

Here's a quick template for you:

Trait

_____

_____

When it didn't work

_____

_____

Remedy

_____

_____

_____

Awareness or indication of improvement

_____

_____

_____

_____

_____

_____

ADMITTED

CHAPTER 7: PREP FOR THE INTERVIEW

Hooray! You've been invited to interview! Many top schools these days require interviews by invitation only, with the notable exceptions of Northwestern's Kellogg School of Management and Dartmouth's Tuck School of Business, which allow open interviews up to a certain date ("Come early and make your case,"

Tuckies say). With most other schools, the process has morphed over the years so that the invitation to interview is almost always an up-or-down indicator of success in the process. The fact that you have been invited to interview is a good sign, and you should feel great that you have made it this far.

Still, the result of the interview is not binary, although it feels like it. It doesn't make sense to be overly nervous, because that won't help your candidacy. But it also doesn't make sense to be overly confident, because that's a turn-off for the interviewer. However, it makes lots of sense to be prepared.

You do not have to redo all the exercises that you've already done in previous chapters to deepen and refine your story. You can draw from what you've already done, including some of the exercises which did not show up directly in the particular school's application. To prepare, review your submitted application and resume and go over the following sections of this workbook:

Work Experience

1. Career Progression: Warm-Up (p. 38)
2. Career Progression: "Why You Do What You Do" (p. 42)
3. One or Two Hero's Model Stories (p. 45)

Essays

1. Influence: "Demonstration of Key Strengths" (p. 85)
2. Leadership: "Emotional IQ" (p. 95)
3. Leadership: "Change and Disappointment" (p. 103)
4. Leadership: "Resiliency" (p. 106)
5. Teamwork (p. 113)

PRACTICE, PRACTICE, PRACTICE

You should also research interview questions you have found on the web. They aren't secrets, and admissions directors expect that you will have done so anyway. As one admissions director said out loud, "It's all fair game."

Before digging into the nitty-gritty questions that you may or may not be asked, take a high-level view. You will find that the interview questions cluster around a few themes: *career goals, why you, why the MBA*, and *why now*?

 EXERCISES

See if you can write down your career goals in three to four sentences. Think big and broaden your vision, but keep your feet on the ground by including the practical steps you might need to take. Note that these goals may overlap with your answers to the "Why You, Why the MBA, Why Now" questions, which come next. That's ok. It's all part of the same story — just don't be repetitive. Although this is an interview about you, I've heard from admissions directors that they want to see that you are aware of the wider world and the realities of living and working in a diverse environment.

Don't memorize what you've written, but practice saying it out loud. Time yourself. About five or six sentences should take about 60 seconds. You probably don't want to go over two minutes or 340 words (at a normal pace).

See if you can write up to a five-sentence (175-word) answer to "What are your career goals?"

_____

_____

_____

_____

_____

_____

_____

_____

_____

_____

_____

_____

_____

_____

_____

_____

See if you can write out a five-sentence answer to "Why you?"

_____

_____

_____

_____

_____

_____

_____

_____

_____

_____

_____

_____

_____

_____

_____

_____

_____

_____

_____

_____

_____

_____

_____

_____

See if you can write out a five-sentence answer to "Why the MBA?"

_____

_____

_____

_____

_____

_____

_____

_____

_____

_____

_____

_____

_____

_____

_____

_____

_____

_____

_____

_____

_____

_____

_____

_____

_____

_____

_____

See if you can write out a five-sentence answer to "Why now?"

_____

_____

_____

_____

_____

_____

_____

_____

_____

_____

_____

_____

_____

_____

_____

_____

_____

_____

_____

_____

_____

_____

_____

_____

Admissions committee members say that succinctness shows confidence. Be succinct but not terse. Practice with friends, on the phone, or record yourself on Skype. Listen to how you sound. Refrain from rambling. Remember, any longer than two minutes and your interviewers may lose focus. Studies show that content represents less than ten percent of delivery (vocal and non-verbal cues constitute the remainder); however, without good content your interview is hollow.

Here's another important answer you want tucked away in your back pocket that interviewers from admissions committees and big consulting firms may ask:

What can you tell me that is *not* on your application and *not* on your resume?

_____

_____

_____

_____

_____

_____

_____

_____

_____

_____

_____

_____

_____

_____

_____

_____

_____

INTERVIEWING THE INTERVIEWER

Almost every interviewer leaves room for questions at the end. You always want to have more questions than you need, and you want them to be good, thoughtful questions. Do not ask questions that can be answered by reading the website; you want to ask questions that require a response from a person. For example, you might ask about the diversity of opinion in the program or for specifics about interaction with faculty.

HELPFUL TIPS

✦ If you've already talked to alumni (and you should have), list any open questions that arose from those conversations.

✦ Ask about a particular professor's course or research and if students can get involved.

✦ Are you interested in trends in the career that appeal to you? Ask about some of the changes the interviewer has seen and if he or she can project what placement might be in that industry two or three years from now.

✦ Run these questions by a friend, advisor, or yes, even an admissions consultant. See if they represent the message you want to present to the school.

List five questions you might want to ask the interviewer.

1. _____

   _____

2. _____

   _____

3. _____

   _____

4. _____

   _____

5. _____

   _____

NUTS AND BOLTS

Technical issues can make or break your interview. The interview is an exercise in preparation. Have you practiced out loud? Make sure you keep practicing and verbalizing. Just writing your answers won't be as effective. Speaking is the only way to make it work. Have you videotaped or recorded yourself?

If you are getting interviewed on Skype or a similar videoconference system, have you tested the technology? Admissions directors have recommended that you get comfortable with videoconferencing and make sure it works properly ahead of your interview.

GET FEEDBACK

We've talked in this workbook quite a bit about giving and receiving feedback. Top business school programs emphasize the give-and-take nature of feedback because it's the best way to learn. Get honest feedback on your interview.

Print out a copy of the following evaluation form for your mock interviewer. Ask him or her to be honest about the areas you can improve on. If you are in a bind, record yourself and answer these questions as objectively as you can, and then repeat the process.

MOCK INTERVIEW EVALUATION FORM

CONTENT

1. Did the interviewee answer the questions?
   ☐ Yes ☐ No

2. Did the interviewee have a positive attitude toward his or her experiences?
   ☐ Yes ☐ No

3. Could you follow the logic of the candidate's answers?
   ☐ Yes ☐ No

4. Did the candidate stay on topic?
   ☐ Yes ☐ No

   If not, did the flow of the discussion suffer?
   ☐ Yes ☐ No

   How would you suggest the interviewee improve the sequence and flow?

   _____

   _____

5. Was the candidate credible?
    ☐ Yes ☐ No

6. Did the interviewee tell stories? ☐ Yes ☐ No

    Were they relevant to leadership and teamwork, even when not asked directly about those two attributes? ☐ Yes ☐ No

7. Was the candidate genuinely enthusiastic about the school?
    ☐ Yes ☐ No

    Did you get the sense that he or she would accept an offer of admission?
    ☐ Yes ☐ No

DELIVERY

1. Was the interviewee grounded?
    ☐ Yes ☐ No

2. Was the interviewee succinct without being terse? ☐ Yes ☐ No
    Did he or she ramble at all? ☐ Yes ☐ No

3. Did the interviewee appear comfortable in his or her body?
    ☐ Yes ☐ No

4. Was the delivery too fast or too slow? Was the pitch too high or too low?
    ☐ Yes ☐ No

5. Was the tone of the interviewee positive and appropriately confident?
    ☐ Yes ☐ No

6. Was his or her language appropriately businesslike and free of jargon or acronyms?
    ☐ Yes ☐ No

7. Was the interviewee likeable? Relaxed enough to have a sense of humor?

☐ Yes   ☐ No

8. Did you get the sense that the interviewee was authentic?

☐ Yes   ☐ No

9. What was the candidate's energy level? How could it be improved?

_____

_____

_____

_____

QUESTIONS TO THE INTERVIEWER

1. Were the questions thoughtful?

☐ Yes   ☐ No

2. Could you tell that the applicant was really interested in the school or just bringing questions along?

☐ Yes   ☐ No

3. Was the applicant knowledgeable about the school?

☐ Yes   ☐ No

4. Were there enough questions to comfortably fill up the time available?

☐ Yes   ☐ No

CHAPTER 8: CONCLUSION: WHAT TO DO WHILE YOU ARE WAITING

As Tom Petty has said: "The waiting is the hardest part." After the intense rush of racing around to meet deadlines, you've suddenly turned in all of your applications. And then you wait.

The waiting comes in stages: first, you think you can ignore it; then it becomes the elephant in the room; and then it becomes the object of prayer/shamanic dances/worry and endlessly clicking the refresh button on your email and the message boards. You also have a hard time making plans: "If I only knew where (or if!) I was going to business school, I would be able to figure out my vacation plans, business travel, whether to adopt a cat, what car to buy, what to have for lunch tomorrow…"

First, make a point of staying sane. You need to do things you enjoy that have nothing to do with work or school. Clear your head, do something non-work related, get back into a decent exercise routine, learn accordion, take apart a motorcycle and put it back together again – anything that you think will keep you from bouncing off walls.

MBA applicants I have known turned to cooking, playing music, training for a road race (on foot or wheels), traveling, or hanging out with family.

One of the admissions officers from Dartmouth's Tuck School of Business wrote a great three-part series on waiting.[5] It contains some great words of wisdom on getting outside of yourself. The blog post's author writes,

> *By putting everything related to B-school applications out of your sight and reconnecting with your interests and hobbies, you ensure that the entirety of your personal horizon is not business school.*

She also suggests helping others who might be struggling with the application process once you are done. But that's for you to decide if you are up for it.

NETWORK IN INDUSTRIES THAT APPEAL

Keep networking with people in the industries in which you think you want to work, because no matter what school you go to, or even if you stay at your current job, learning about other opportunities will expand your horizons. The other advantage of being in limbo is that you can interview people in different industries without the pressure of actually looking for a job.

---

[5] 🖱 http://tuckschool.blogspot.com/2010/01/what-to-do-while-youre-waiting-pt-1.html

MAKING THE CHOICE BETWEEN TWO OR MORE SCHOOLS

As an admissions consultant, I love talking with people about their happy choices. With luck, you *will* have to make such a choice. And it will never be a choice among equals because all things are never equal. Location, family/ employer/friends' opinions, financial aid, the job market, and your mood at the moment will all converge. There's no wrong answer. Enjoy it — choosing between two or more of your target programs is a wonderful problem to have.

The Knight Management Center, Stanford Graduate School of Business

If it doesn't work out as you hope, the world will not end. But that's not why you are reading this book. You are reading and working through it because you have big dreams. You want to know that you have done the very best that you could in putting together a top-notch application. You want to know you couldn't have done more. That by itself should feel pretty darn good.

Good luck, keep in touch with your old friends, and always stay authentic. The world is waiting.

ADMITTED

150

ACKNOWLEDGEMENTS

It all started with Bill Hogan, who coached me on six successful MBA applications and encouraged me to write this book. I'd also like to thank for inspiration Stacey Aaronson, Francesca Di Meglio, Heidi Pickman, Meadow DeVor, Alice Woodman-Russell, Helen Rothbaum, and Leila Pirnia of MBA Podcaster. My life would be so much different without 85 Broads — Meghan Doherty, Krista Sande-Kerbeck and the fabulous Janet Hanson. A big hug also to Doug Barg of Kaplan for his long-term support and Barbara Mark, for telling me to just get it done. Thank you also to the incredibly knowledgeable colleagues who have served with me in AIGAC, particularly Candy LaBalle of MBA Spain. Finally, thanks to the whole extended family, on two and four legs; you all know who you are, especially my very best friend.

~ Betsy

I'd like to thank my husband Antonio Gerenini for putting up with me as I fiddle away my days working on projects, such as this book, and our baby, who was in the womb during this assignment, and serves as the ultimate motivation to do great things both personally and professionally. My editors past and present, parents, Pasquale and Regina, my brother John, sister Rosaria, sister-in-law Jaci, and niece Maria deserve thanks, too, for all they do to help me grow. Most of all, I'd like to thank Betsy, the mastermind behind this book and a smart professional with tons of patience. She is one of a kind, and this book is a credit to her dedication.

~ Francesca

ADMITTED

ABOUT THE AUTHORS

ABOUT THE AUTHORS

Betsy Massar is founder of Master Admissions, a graduate admissions consulting firm specializing in MBA applications. Her passion for business school admissions comes from her own experience applying to and attending Harvard Business School, and then following the Wall Street path to Goldman Sachs and several other surviving investment firms. From 1988 to 1998 she lived in Taiwan, Singapore and Hong Kong, where she taught, wrote for the financial press, worked for a local private equity firm, and sold securities to major institutional investors. Since returning to the US, she has worked as a journalist and marketer in the San Francisco Bay Area. She has been a critical analytical communications coach at the Stanford Graduate School of Business and is an active member of 85 Broads. Betsy serves on the board of the Association of International Graduate Admissions Consultants (AIGAC).

Francesca Di Meglio is a freelance journalist based in northern New Jersey. An expert on business schools, she has spent more than seven years covering all things management education, with particular emphasis on MBA admissions, rankings, curriculum, and careers. In addition, Di Meglio is the Guide to Newlyweds for About.com, and maintains the Two Worlds website about Italian American life and culture. Her stories have appeared in numerous publications and websites, including MBA Jungle, Ladies' Home Journal, and Monster.com.

153

ADMITTED

INDEX

PHOTO CREDITS

p. 7   Jamie Dimon, photo courtesy of World Economic Forum

p. 37   Photograph by Lewis Hine, 1920

p. 64   Dalai Lama, photograph by Luca Galuzzi

p. 69   Muhammad Ali, photo courtesy of the Library of Congress

p. 79   Oprah Winfrey, photograph by Alan Light

p. 107   Michael Jordan, photograph by Steve Lipofsky

p. 113   Discovery Space Shuttle Team, photo courtesy of NASA

NOTES

NOTES

NOTES

NOTES

NOTES

NOTES

NOTES

NOTES

NOTES

NOTES

85Broads

www.85broads.com

85 Broads is a global women's network whose mission is to generate exceptional professional and social value for its members. Through our regional network events and online at 85Broads.com, members invest their time, their intellect, and their financial capital in each other's ideas and businesses.

85 Broads was founded in 1997 as a network for current and former Goldman Sachs women who worked at **85 Broad Street**, the firm's NYC headquarters, and at other GS offices worldwide. In 2000, at the urging of women at Harvard Business School, we expanded the network to include women who were students and alumnae of the world's leading graduate business schools, irrespective of chosen career path.

In 2004, we recognized the importance of further expanding the network to include women at the undergraduate level who were pursuing every career path imaginable. Over the next three years, we created campus clubs at 40 colleges in the US and abroad.

And in 2007, we extended membership in 85 Broads to **all amazing, trailblazing women worldwide** without regard to one's college or graduate school affiliation. The women in 85 Broads are entrepreneurs, investment bankers, consultants, filmmakers, lawyers, educators, athletes, venture capitalists, portfolio managers, political leaders, philanthropists, doctors, engineers, artists, and scientists, in addition to women who are seeking to blaze new trails.

Membership Benefits:

Online services: access to the profiles and email addresses of 30,000 members worldwide through our Advanced Member Search, company SPOTLIGHT pages, Job Board, Events Calendar, Blogs, Videos from past events, Jam Sessions on hot topics, and a variety of social media tools.

Offline services: exclusive regional chapter events and on-campus events at member colleges and universities.

Our Campus Presence:

85 Broads has student members at hundreds of undergraduate and graduate schools worldwide. Our campus clubs host conferences on topics of interest including wealth management, career development, and ways to live your most empowered life! They also provide a forum for our undergraduate and graduate school members to develop and hone their leadership skills, which dramatically increases their lifetime "return" on their education.

85 Broads Chapters:

Our Regional Chapters develop and strengthen our global presence through exclusive workshops and events featuring industry and career experts. New chapters are created at our members' request and are organized and run by members of the network who passionately believe in the value of investing in, and learning from, smart women - from student to senior executive - globally. 85 Broads has active chapters in the following locations:

Domestic:

Atlanta, GA	Minneapolis/St. Paul, MN
Austin, TX	New York City, NY
Boston, MA	Northern California
Chicago, IL	Philadelphia, PA
Cincinnati, OH	Phoenix, AZ
Dallas, TX	Pittsburgh, PA
Denver, CO	Seattle, WA
Detroit, MI	Southern California
Fairfield/Westchester(NY/CT)	Washington DC
Miami, FL	

International:

Beijing, China

Dubai, UAE

Hong Kong, China

Hyderabad, India

Istanbul, Turkey

Lisbon, Portugal

London, UK

Madrid, Spain

Milan, Italy

Mumbai, India

São Paulo, Brazil

Scandinavia

Seoul, South Korea

Shanghai, China

Singapore

Southern Africa

Learn More about 85 Broads:

Information: www.85broads.com/who_we_are

Application: www.85broads.com/welcome

Facebook: https://www.facebook.com/pages/85-Broads/25558491898

Twitter: @85broads

Email: info@85broads.com

MBA IQ

The MBA IQ: The Prep Course for the MBA Classroom

The MBA IQ® prepares you for the MBA classroom. First impressions take seconds to form – make a great one. You did a lot to prepare for admission. You invested a lot of time and energy into your job, grades, the GMAT, writing resumes, and securing great recommendations. Make sure you don't show up on your first day unprepared. Invest the time to succeed in the classroom.

Why is The MBA IQ so important as part of your MBA path?

* Business school is competitive – grades do matter
* Knowing the language of business is an important step in your career – master the MBA Lexicon™ in order to accelerate your academic ramp-up time
* Gain the confidence to compete in the classroom and the workplace – do not get left behind
* Be able to jump into group work, social life, and career exploration by showing up with a foundation to build upon

MBA IQ was founded in 2010 by Devi Vallabhaneni and Melissa Hayes, both Harvard Business School MBAs. The duo developed a unique approach to preparing prospective MBAs for the rigors of a MBA program by teaching them a comprehensive business lexicon. They launched the program because of their MBA experiences.

"We found HBS to be an incredibly rewarding experience – from the case studies to the cold calls – and wanted to be able to share that knowledge with others. We believe that the more prepared you are for the MBA classroom, the more you benefit from MBA academics."

- Devi and Melissa

The MBA IQ offers one of the few MBA preparation curricula focusing on <u>the entire foundation of MBA programs</u>. Most mini-MBA courses out there only focus on a handful of topics such as basic finance and accounting. The MBA IQ covers the following 12 Learning Modules:

- General Management, Leadership, and Strategy
- Operations Management
- Marketing Management
- Quality and Process Management
- Human Resources Management
- Accounting
- Finance
- Information Technology
- Corporate Control, Law, Ethics, and Governance
- International Business
- Project Management
- Decision Sciences & Managerial Economics

Where the program truly stands apart is with the one-of-a-kind MBA IQ Score, which makes the MBA IQ program the first to actually calculate one's level of business knowledge. Just as a FICO score indicates one's financial health, the MBA IQ Score is an accurate indicator of one's business knowledge. The MBA IQ Score is given as an overall score as well as a score in each of the twelve foundational areas of business.

Many "mini MBA" courses can run hundreds or even thousands of dollars. The MBA IQ program is only $195. For more information, visit:

www.mbaiq.com

Made in the USA
Lexington, KY
19 February 2012